WALLACE

Portrait of William Wallace reproduced by Schenck and McFarlane of Edinburgh from an original reputedly sold by Cromwell out of the English Royal Collection of Charles I; courtesy of Renfrew District Council (Paisley Museum).

PETER REESE

WALLACE

A Biography

CANONGATE

For Barbara, my wife

First published in Great Britain in
1996 by Canongate Books Ltd,
14 High Street, Edinburgh

Reprinted 1996 and 1997

ISBN 0 86241 607 8

British Library Cataloguing-in-publication Data
A catalogue record for this book is available
on request from the British Library

Typeset by Hewer Text Composition Services,
Edinburgh
Printed and bound in Finland by WSOY

CONTENTS

The Scottish Succession

as it relates to the main claimants in the Great Cause of 1291-92

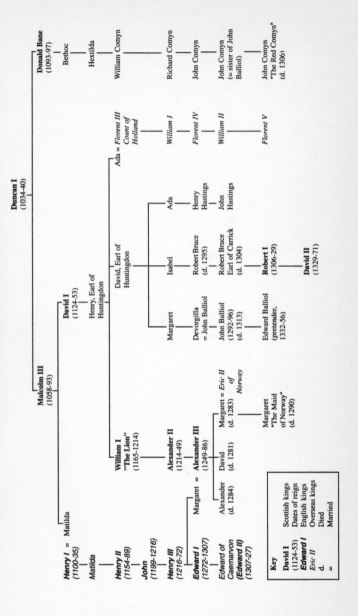

Key

David I (1124-53)	Scottish kings / Dates of reign
Edward I	English kings
Eric II	Overseas kings
d.	Died
=	Married

ACKNOWLEDGEMENTS

IN THE DAYS BEFORE many dual-carriage roads or extensive motorways, whenever I drove to the far north I would break my journey at Stirling. After long hours in a car I relished climbing up to the Castle from where I would gaze across the wide plain intersected by the shimmering Forth towards the dark prominence of Abbey Craig topped by its great monument. As I repeated the ritual I became ever more determined to learn about the man it commemorated.

For the germ of an idea to become a published work I owe very much to many people. The staffs of the British Library, the National Library of Scotland, the Edinburgh Central Library and Stirling Reference Library have been most helpful. The text was largely written in my second home, the Prince Consort's Military Library, Aldershot, and I would like to thank the present librarian, Mr Tim Ward; the Army's Systems librarian, Mr Paul Vickers, who has also produced excellent battle plans, maps and tables; Mrs Alice Alexander; Mrs Linda Surman; Mrs Pam Parker; Mrs Jean Duffield; Mrs Gail Ward and Mrs Elaine Edwards.

At St Andrews University I benefited from Ronald Cant's deep knowledge and ageless enthusiasm; in Edinburgh Professor Geoffrey Barrow was kind enough to discuss William Wallace with me and to appear persuaded that another biography of the great man was not unreasonable; at Falkirk, archeologist Geoffrey Bailey and local historian John Walker fielded my many queries on the battle of Falkirk and at Bridge of Allan Craig Mair helped me straighten out some of my ideas and much else besides.

In England my old and valued friend Dr Leslie Wayper

reacted in his inimitable fashion to concepts yet unformed; Mrs Jennifer Prophet did wonders for the style and, together with her son Charles, produced the index, while Colonel Mike Wellings gave me his honest and clear reactions. Mrs Christine Batten put her word processor to wonderful effect transforming idiosyncratic handwriting into a legible form and then amended things more times than I like to remember.

I am greatly indebted to my publisher Hugh Andrew of Canongate Books for taking up the script of an Englishman who dared to write about one of Scotland's greatest heroes; Dr Richard Oram as historical editor, Neville Moir who brought the text to the production stage and Duncan McAra as textual editor.

Any shortcomings are, of course, mine alone.

Peter Reese

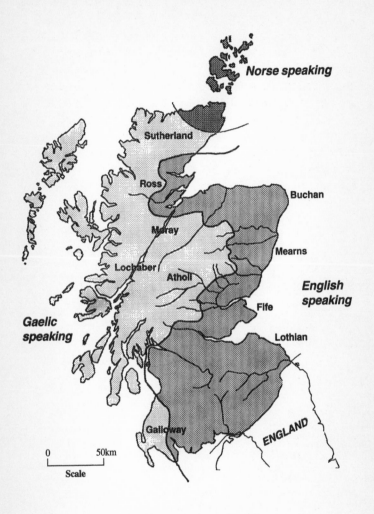

Norse speaking

Sutherland

Ross

Buchan

Moray

Mearns

Lochaber

Atholl

English speaking

Fife

Gaelic speaking

Lothian

ENGLAND

Galloway

0   50km

Scale

Scotland: Language Division

■ Lyne — Roman Fort
○ Bellie — Roman marching camp
◑ *Dumfries* — Modern town
PICTI — Tribe
— Roads
- - - Route to the north

Roman Scotland

Scottish Medieval Burghs

≈

STIRLING REMEMBERS

'Still is thy name in high account.'
Sir Walter Scott

ON 23 JUNE 1861 it was raining in Stirling, whose towering castle had often barred invaders venturing northwards, and in whose vicinity two battles vital to the independence of Scotland had taken place. But by mid-morning the sun broke through and it turned out clear and dry, with that pleasing freshness that often follows heavy rain. Townsfolk on the castle rock, gazing at Abbey Craig two miles away had no difficulty in making out the sharp outlines and different shades of green among the trees covering that lesser but still dominant outcrop. The weather was fortunate, for large numbers of people were on their way to the burgh. Their purpose this time was not to oppose English invaders but to take part in a great celebration. That afternoon many of them, in all manner of formal dress, would march from the town to Abbey Craig. Once there they were due to take part in a ceremony to commemorate their great compatriot William Wallace who, almost 564 years before, brought his men rushing down that hill to defeat a superior English army as it crossed the meandering but wide river Forth.

The Victorians loved to erect triumphal monuments and statues and Stirling was in festive mood. Wreaths of evergreens topped by a royal standard hung across its main thoroughfare, Murray Place, while in the village of Causewayhead, between Stirling and Abbey Craig, where in Wallace's time most invading armies passed northwards, a wooden arch had been built.

This was also decked with evergreens and surmounted by two flagstaffs. As day-excursion trains pulled into Stirling station travellers found it decorated with flags and other emblems while outside two medals struck to commemorate the event were on sale. While not everyone could afford the medals, all could mingle with their fellow onlookers and share a sense of growing excitement heightened by the proud strains of military bands. There was, too, the clopping of horses' hooves mingled with the rattle of their harnesses, while seemingly from every corner came the measured tread of marching feet.

In other nearby towns, such as Alloa and Falkirk and in Stirling's neighbouring villages on both sides of the Forth, business activity came to a halt. In many cases those involved in the festivities had declared local holidays, to release others who wanted to watch. In addition to those travelling by train people came by road, riding in horse omnibuses decorated with evergreens, in farmers' carts, on horseback or on foot. More than 80,000 visitors converged on a town where the population was just 10,000 and its neighbouring villages often had less than two hundred people.

All knew that they were marking the memory of an outstanding Scottish hero, even if to many his deeds were but sketchily known. Most were aware he had gained a great victory against the English invaders near Abbey Craig. Wasn't this where the foundation stone of the monument would be laid? But details about an event so long ago were scarce. Only the better-informed understood how Wallace's victory had gained precious time for Robert Bruce to emerge to pick up the sword and subsequently defeat the English at nearby Bannockburn. The connection between Wallace's victory at Stirling Bridge and Scotland's continuing independence for the best part of 400 years until, by the Act of Union (1707), it could join its larger neighbour with its traditions intact, was not immediately obvious. In any case for many attending, however patriotic, the historical details were less important than the spectacle which was to come. For the vast majority, it was the great procession to Abbey Craig which was *the* event, scheduled to set off from the King's park under the joint command of Lt-General Sir James Maxwell Wallace (a descendent of the hero), Captain J.T. Roehead, the engineer officer who had designed the Gothic monument and Chief Constable Meffen. The leaders were to be followed by 25,000 uniformed men from all parts of Scotland – two and a half times the number of Wallace's compatriots who attacked the English at Stirling Bridge.

At one o'clock the firing of a single gun from the castle ramparts signalled the order to move, while at the same time the bells of Stirling's churches rang out. Sir James Maxwell Wallace, the Grand Marshal, together with his two deputies (all three resplendently dressed) stepped off accompanied by 'a large instrumental band'. They were followed directly by twenty-seven different companies of military volunteers, all with their own pipers. The last of these was the ancient society of the Stirling Omnium Gatherum. Their members were mounted on garlanded plough-horses similar in build to those used by the proud English knights who clattered across Stirling's narrow bridge to attack Wallace over five centuries before. Next came a lighter note, eighteen curling clubs, nine Gardeners' lodges and six St Crispin lodges in their odd dress, most accompanied by musicians. Then followed the representatives of the twenty-one municipal bodies and other civic officers who preceded the master gunner of Dumbarton Castle. He had been given the honour of carrying Wallace's sword, fully 5ft 7in long, the symbol of his power which had been lodged in Dumbarton Castle since Wallace's own time, together with that of King Robert Bruce.

In final place came masonic lodges from all over Scotland, 138 in all, and last of all their Worshipful Grand Master, the Duke of Atholl. It took fully two hours before the Grand Lodge emerged upon the summit of Abbey Craig some 360 ft above the surrounding countryside.

The laying of the foundation stone of what would become a 220ft-high tower was accompanied by a divine blessing and a masonic dedication involving 'mystic rite and solemn ceremony'. This finished with various bands striking up 'The Merry Masons' followed by 'God save the Queen'. It was now time for speeches to be made in a wooden pavilion specially erected there for the purpose. These attempted to outdo each other in their tributes to those responsible for the celebration and, of course, to the cause of it all, the hero himself. It was no time for understatement. The Revd Dr Charles Rogers, secretary of the Wallace Monument Committee and main force behind the movement for a national monument raised by public subscription, started things off by congratulating the members of the Wallace family in the following terms: 'We are celebrating the memory of a chief who made Scotland a nation, placed a new dynasty on the English throne and under Providence was the means of uniting these kingdoms in equal terms and with equal rights.'

Later the leading participants attended a grand banquet held in the Corn Exchange, where 350 gentlemen sat down to dinner. Ladies were required to eat in a separate gallery at the west end of the building. The feast was followed by the inevitable toasts, seventeen in all, together with their responses, the premier one being the loyal toast 'to the joint monarch of both countries, the Queen, other members of the Royal Family, the Armed Forces and the volunteers'.

A degree of self-interest was clearly apparent. It was doubtful whether most Scottish masons were ardent admirers of Wallace, but as chief celebrant at Stirling their leader was able to demonstrate the masons' contemporary influence across Scotland. And after the Revd Gillan resung the praises he had paid Wallace on the previous evening he made a distinctly forced allusion to the way that Wallace's beliefs had led to the emergence of the covenanting movement. He was followed by Professor Blackie, champion of the Celtic revival who, while acknowledging Wallace as the preserver of Scotland's independence, felt, in a way best known to himself, that the great Lowlander concurred with Blackie's own mission – in reviving that country's Highland customs and Celtic traditions.

By 1861 the countries had been united for 150 years. While the volunteers who marched to Abbey Craig showed a continuing martial spirit, the arms they carried were for a great empire whose capital was in London. And the efforts by Professor Blackie to revive all things Scottish, especially the Celtic traditions of the Highlands, had a markedly antiquarian stamp about them. Some who attended at Stirling must have realised that the very material and technological advances which helped to bring great numbers of spectators there could just as easily be used to carry ever-increasing numbers of English visitors. And that such invaders, peaceful as they were, represented the latest challenge to the distinctness of their country and to its characteristic values.

How far Scotland, saved by Wallace from subservience in 1297, has succeeded in retaining its national identity, is for the book's concluding chapters to discuss. Before then its concern is with Wallace, the man and his achievements, the human figure behind the shadowy stereotypes produced by the speakers at Stirling. Curiosity about him has, of course, scarcely been confined to ceremonies connected with his memorials. In the case of a national hero such as Wallace there will always be some allegorisation, interpretation and reinterpretation of his life. From the eighteenth century onwards for instance, a stream of biographers has taken him as their subject. Understandably the approaches taken by different authors vary widely. One of the later writers, Sir James Fergusson, was determined to confine himself to sources which could be verified (which he then construed). This led him to refer scathingly to the eighteenth and nineteenth century accounts with their 'embellishments and distortions'.[1] And during the eighteenth century the versions by Abercromby[2] and Crawford[3] with their archaic treatment, complete with illustrations of Gothic ruins and family armour, were undeniably romantic. In the following century came the High Victorian viewpoint of Dr Charles Rogers[4] and the bold certainty of that later Victorian writer A.F. Murison.[5] With the moderns we have a more austere approach, notably by Sir James Fergusson and a writer of the late twentieth century, Andrew Fisher.[6] In contrast D.J. Gray's biography[7] published in 1991 re-adopts something of the heroic approach and four years later we have James Mackay's biography,[8] the longest so far, which among other things comes to new conclusions about Wallace's birthplace. The present book will hardly be the last to be written about him.

CHAPTER ONE

≈

WALLACE'S SCOTLAND

'And when you, Scotland, had been headless and
unable to defend yourself, Wallace had appeared
as a mighty arm for you and a salvation in time
of trouble.'

Walter Bower, Scotichronicon

THOSE VICTORIAN DIGNITARIES AT Stirling who struggled
to identify the man behind the Wallace legend were not
alone; anyone interested in Wallace faces the same problems,
namely the intervening centuries, the limited evidence about
his life, the nature of the writings about him relatively shortly
after his death (inevitably affected by the attention paid to
the greater historical figure of King Robert I), and the
different approaches taken by his later biographers. Among
the religious chroniclers of his day, for instance, there are
the flattering accounts by Scots in the *Scotichronicon* with
its patriotic contributors John of Fordun and Walter Bower,
opposed vigorously by the English viewpoint, the 'outlaw and
brigand school', expressed by Walter of Hemingburgh and
Matthew of Westminster. Along with this group are the
various contributors within the Priory of Lanercost who
invariably portrayed Wallace as a monster. Things would
change for the better if only two contemporary accounts
could be rediscovered, the biography written by his personal
chaplain, John Blair, of which only fragments remain, and an
account of his life made by Thomas Gray, parson of Liberton,
which is completely missing. After nearly 700 years such wishes
are surely in vain.

Difficulties in trying to discover the true Wallace are

exacerbated because of the 'image' presented in the most famous account of him, despite its author's claims that it was based on John Blair's biography. Close on 200 years after Wallace's death Henry the Minstrel (Blind Harry) wrote a 400-page account – all in rhyming couplets – in which he skilfully interwove popular accounts and hearsay with real events to produce a work which not only celebrated Wallace but reflected the anti-English sentiments of Harry's own day. Stirring and immensely popular as this account was it cannot be considered impartial or accurate in matters of detail, although it unquestionably made use of the folklore which had gathered about Wallace. One of the most dispassionate of Harry's contemporaries, the Scottish historian John Major, struck a timely note of caution about its historical validity: 'There was one Henry, blind by birth, who in the time of my childhood, fabricated a whole book about William Wallace, and therein he wrote down in our native rhymes – and this was a kind of composition in which he had much skill – all that passed current among the people in his day. I, however, can give but a partial credence to such writings as these . . .'[1] Despite John Major's scepticism it is unlikely that the Rhymer, who earned his living by narrating before men of the highest rank, made factual errors owing to his being blind from birth. When he wrote his account he probably still had his sight. John Major himself attributed some of Harry's glaring chronological errors to his reciting his work in parts. (It was, of course, far too long to be related in only one sitting.) And when Harry came to old age – and was certainly blind – he might well have forgotten some of the true details and their historical sequence.[2] Notwithstanding, there is more hard evidence available on William Wallace than any other commander in the Scottish Wars of Independence, even Wallace's co-leader at the battle of Stirling Bridge, Andrew Moray.

By whatever means people become acquainted with William Wallace they naturally want to come to their own assessment of him. With someone who lived seven centuries ago they can hardly do so without some understanding of his society and a glimpse of the primary colours, at least, which helped to make up that vivid and intricate tapestry which was Wallace's Scotland.

Territorially thirteenth-century Scotland resembled modern Scotland, excluding Orkney and Shetland. This was a recent development for it was only in 1263, after the battle of Largs, that the Hebrides had finally been taken from the king of Norway, while just thirty years before, in 1237, the demarcation of the Scottish border had been recognised through a treaty made between England and Scotland and sealed at York. The treaty effectively ended Scottish claims to the northernmost regions of England (the old counties of Cumberland and Northumberland), and English claims to a Northumberland stretching into Lothian Scotland.

Constitutionally Scotland was a long-established kingdom which had preceded the Norman succession in England (see table of The Scottish Succesion on p. vi). In 1034 five distinct regions (the Norwegian north-west was still excluded) had been brought under one Celtic ruler, Duncan I, a descendant of the royal family of the Scots. Before the succession crisis of 1286, which heralded the Wars of Independence and Wallace's contribution to history, the same vigorous dynasty had governed Scotland for over 250 years.

In this respect Scotland differed markedly from Wales – also threatened by an expansionist English monarchy – where no royal line had gained comparable ascendancy and there was continuing rivalry between the princes of the north and south for control of the principality. Within the kingdom of Scotland there were many different nationalities – Picts, Scots, Britons, Angles, Norwegians and Flemings – with their different languages and different racial and cultural traditions, living in markedly different geographical regions.

For simplicity, thirteenth-century Scotland can be seen as Caesar looked at Gaul, by dividing it into three parts: the south-east, the north-west and a central area stretching upwards from Galloway in the extreme south-west to the flat land of Caithness in the far north-east. In the south-east, in Lothian, the predominant language was northern English (with Norman French the language of the court and the greater nobles); in the north-west the languages were Gaelic and Norse, while in the central area the situation was much more complicated. In the hill lands of Galloway, for instance, Gaelic was the predominant tongue, but, in the rich agricultural areas of the north-east, English was spreading quickly at the expense of the native Gaelic. Between these two extremes there were surprising admixtures of races and languages (see map of Scotland's Languages on p. ix), with Flemish joining the others in places where Flemish merchants (after oppression in the Low Countries) had been made welcome by the Scots kings.

In the late thirteenth century Scottish nobles had to be multilingual with knowledge of Gaelic, English and Norman French, while the common people were as likely as not to have some knowledge of a second language, probably some English or Flemish in addition to Gaelic, or, in the case of the south-east, some Gaelic to supplement their English. William Wallace and Robert Bruce, for instance, would have grown up at least bilingual, speaking French and English (with some knowledge of Latin). Robert probably had a sound knowledge of Gaelic from his upbringing in the intensely Celtic society of Carrick, while Wallace may have acquired familiarity with the tongue.

The different races that made up the realm of Scotland were revealed in the early twelfth century when, at the battle of the Standard, King David I led a Scottish host into northern England. In his army there were Norman knights (owning Scottish estates), Angle footsoldiers from Lothian, Celts from the north, Norse Gaels from the north-west, Norwegians from Caithness and Orkney, and Galwegians from Galloway.

Apparently 'they all quarrelled and jostled and insulted one another in at least four languages' and not for the last time lost to the English as a result.[3]

Scotland's population in the late thirteenth century, amounting to about 400,000, was a mixture of assorted peoples, distinguishable by their favoured tongue, appearance, temperament and aspirations. That being said it was a country where the majority language was still Gaelic and where its peoples, despite their different origins, took pride in its Celtic nature as a conscious bond and symbol of their nationhood.

However, from the eleventh century onwards, particularly after the accession of the Normans to the English throne, Scottish kings came to favour the superior Norman system both in central government and their civil administration. Within their own households they established the three separate offices of steward, chancellor and chamberlain and then applied the same principles across the country. The thirteen great earls (harking back to the earlier Celtic mormaors), who traditionally had an influential share in the government of the country, were still there but their roles were reduced. Over the country as a whole the kings appointed three senior officials as their chief administrative and judicial officers, one being responsible for the area north of the Firth and Clyde, one for Lothian and the third for Galloway. While they might well be earls, more importantly their authority came directly from the crown. Under these came another twenty-six royal officers, sheriffs, whose sheriffdoms or units of authority ignored traditional land divisions. Such men with their wide powers over legal, financial and administrative matters supplanted the functionaries under the earlier Celtic kings.

The Scottish kings also adopted the feudal system of land ownership whereby all men held their lands and property through the consent of their superior lord, the king. Although this was not general, with the western Highlands being less affected than elsewhere, and not as firmly based in the south of the country as in England, it unquestionably strengthened their hold over the state.[4] This gave them the opportunity, for instance, to call upon certain Norman barons to help fight their old enemies in the far north, if they challenged the king's authority. Such a policy was not without its dangers. As a reward, some of them, such as the Bruces and Baliols, acquired extensive estates in southern Scotland which, together with beneficial marriages to Scottish noblewomen, raised them into positions of leading contenders for the throne. One hardly needs to emphasise the serious problems for Scotland, the nation, from such 'deep aristocratic penetration' by men who still owed allegiance to an English king for their estates south of the border.[5]

However, while such Norman systems might help the Scottish royal house to confirm its hold over the country, during the first half of the thirteenth century relations with the English were generally friendly and its representatives never considered their smaller kingdom was somehow becoming ripe for incorporation with Norman England. Scottish kings certainly sent their younger sons to the English court where they were given English names, took English wives and learned to adopt Norman customs, but the English influence was far from paramount. The Scottish royal family also gave its daughters as brides to the Low Countries, Norway and Brittany, and took brides from France and Flanders, as well as from England. Most important of all, despite the country's racial mixture and its kings' decision to adopt Norman administrative practices, the 'community of the realm of Scotland' – as it first came to be called in the thirteenth century – possessed a distinctive political and cultural tradition of its own. This sense of such a kingdom – that could even subsist for a time without a king – went far beyond the common features of the feudal 'system' which Scotland shared with England and much of north-western Europe. King Alexander III, for instance, who was still enthroned at the traditional Celtic location of Scone, was proud to have his family's genealogy presented in the traditional Celtic way and recited to him in Gaelic.

During the thirteenth century the feeling of separate nation-hood grew as the country's affairs flourished under two strong kings, Alexander II (1214–49) and Alexander III (1249–86). Their relations with the English monarchy were good, even cordial on occasions, and there seemed no need for English kings to press questions concerning their degree of overlordship of Scotland. If anything, the internal distinctions between the two countries widened as feudalism in Scotland developed its particular practices, as for that matter feudalism was doing elsewhere. The polyglot nature of the Scottish people (and the different languages which they spoke) led their kings to adopt a common language for administrative purposes. For this they chose northern English, the native language of Lothian, the region which was increasingly becoming the country's economic and political centre of gravity. English was chosen in preference to French, the predominant language of both the English court and the main currency of the feudal system. As a result English (rather than French) made rapid strides, especially in the towns and within the church, although Gaelic retained its place as the most commonly spoken language of a proudly Celtic country.

Differences in the feudal practices within Scotland were real enough. For instance, the system in the far north was much more complicated than elsewhere and great family chiefs ruled over their clansmen in demi-kingdoms, largely uninterrupted by royal officials. It would be wrong, though, to assume that, despite different systems of land tenure in this area, they necessarily acted against the power of their overlord, the king. In Moray there were men who proudly bore the title 'the freemen of Moray': they had been granted land rights by the king himself in return for military service and such men recognised that their final allegiance was to the king.

Not only in Moray but across Scotland as a whole men tended to have greater freedom than in the rest of Europe. This applied not only to the great provincial lords or the proud rulers of Galloway and Argyll but to many in the close-knit burghs and on royal estates in Lothian and Strathclyde. Many Scottish estates were smaller than elsewhere and land was often held by men of fairly small substance. Such men, perhaps tenants in chief or guidmen whose land had been granted by one of the great magnates, could hardly be so far removed in rank from the townsfolk, lesser freemen or the peasantry, as many seigneurial lords were in England.

Except for the premier families the majority of Scottish nobles tended to be less wealthy than those south of the border. In time of war the numbers of knights which they could bring to the king's summons hardly ever exceeded five and were often down to one or two. As for the larger estates where the principals were often absent, their affairs were likely to be left in the hands of a tacksman who came from local stock.[6] He could scarcely hold himself aloof. With those areas of the country where feudalism hardly applied or where it had not taken a full hold there were a relatively large number of small yeoman farmers and free labourers. Even where it did operate a steady number of husbandmen were – with their overlord's co-operation – already commuting their feudal obligations into cash payments. As Ranald Nicholson put it, 'There were far more intermediate stages along the feudal pyramid than in England'.[7] This significant proportion of free men were frequently self-confident, proud and robust individuals.

As a result a strong sense of individuality and love of freedom had grown up, a quality accentuated by the country's geographical characteristics. Some localities were always difficult to penetrate and almost totally inaccessible during the winter. As a result even more than in England external events tended to have a limited effect on their inhabitants' pattern of life.

Whilst the king and his senior officers, strongly escorted and using relays of fresh horses, could enforce their will across the country, it was much more difficult for lesser officials and other travellers to penetrate certain regions, especially the mountainous ones. In any event Scottish kings never attempted to raise taxes as frequently as English ones and, unlike England, its parliaments were not attended by representatives of all the territorial communities nor did the country have a central court of justice. Unlike England, Scotland was never long under the centralising influence of Roman rule and had not been opened up by their great trunk roads. After Edinburgh (Cramond) the main artery to the extreme north ran up the eastern side of the country via Aberdeen to a point on the north coast short of Inverness. In places it was hardly more than a basic track relying on upturned turfs rather than more durable layers of stone (see map of Roman Scotland on p. x.) Not only did extensive woodlands render large areas of the central regions all but inaccessible, but in the north, hill ranges produced the same results, while in the north-west Highlands the heavily indented coastline with both its mountains and great lochs caused what were never more than tracks to be few and far between. In any case even what passed for roads were liable to peter out when they reached the high passes or crossed desolate moors. An indication of such poor land communications was the greater reliance placed on seaborne traffic than in England. It was customary for furs and skins to be carried out of small north-western ports such as Aultbea and Gairloch to Inverness where they were often transhipped to Aberdeen rather than carried across wild country where tracks relied on stepping stones over fast-flowing rivers and bands of fierce marauders were ever likely to lie in wait.

Such geographical and climatic considerations led the Scottish rulers to deviate from their English counterparts in another way, too. Scotland, like England, was predominantly a rural country. Yet, owing to its comparative remoteness and large areas of bare hill and moorland which contributed little to the royal revenues, together with the untamed nature of the people who lived in such localities, the Scottish kings sponsored urban communities to a much greater extent than south of the border. So-called free burghs were given the privilege of being called royal. This was to distinguish them from the smaller number of towns where similar concessions were granted by the church or by barons such as Robert Bruce at Annandale or James the Steward at Renfrew. Those living in the royal burghs enjoyed a number of significant privileges. They were granted special rights with regard to trading and land ownership and allowed to choose their bailies, hold their own courts and to collect their own revenues. In return they paid a stipulated sum direct to the king who also benefited from collecting customs fees on the burgh's goods destined for export. During the thirteenth century thirty-six of the fifty towns given burgh status were royal burghs although the main expansion had occurred in the preceding century under King David I (1124–53) who granted twenty-five such charters (see map of Scottish Medieval Burghs on p. xi).

The burghs played a greater part in the country's economy than their size suggested. They not only swelled the royal treasury but extended the king's power. The 'burgesses' of the royal burghs tended to be strongly loyal to the crown, while their towns' commercial development helped to increase its prestige. Most of the royal burghs were either on the east coast or sent their produce through east coast ports. Among their inhabitants were merchants and craftsmen from eastern England, Flanders and the Rhineland as well as native Scots. Berwick was a supreme example where its Flemish merchants repaid the royal bounty of sanctuary by developing it into the richest trading centre in Scotland. While trading and revenue were the main motives, there were other reasons for granting such privileges; Dumfries was made a royal burgh partly in the hope of developing some sense of order and responsibility among the wild Galwegians there. Similar thinking lay behind the creation of a royal burgh at Dingwall on the fringes of the rugged north-west. In such townships English was the language used for commercial transactions but, as most burghs faced east, their trading interests were more with the Continent than with England. This can be better appreciated when one realises that the burgh of Aberdeen was 'as close to the Elbe as the Thames and closer to Norway than either'.[8]

Burghs helped to emphasise the individuality of Scotland as a nation in yet another way. They reinforced the trend for individuals to gain their freedom. If serfs who had fled from the feudal estates remained unchallenged for a year and a day they became free men. A steady number apparently found refuge in such fiercely independent communities and, after gaining their freedom, tended to stay on to play a full part.

Yet probably above all else it was the Scottish church that accentuated the distinctness of the two kingdoms and, hardly surprisingly, it took an important part in opposing the English invaders during the independence wars. Two major ecclesiastical reforms had been instituted by King David I during the previous century. While under the easy-going Celtic church many older pagan traditions continued and religious rites varied from area to area, this was changed when the whole country, including the far north, was divided into ecclesiastical units – dioceses – each under its own bishop. Four early bishoprics, St Andrews, Dunkeld, Moray and Glasgow, were joined by five more: Ross, Aberdeen, Caithness, Dunblane and Brechin. Twelve Scottish bishops were consecrated under papal arrangements, taking their religious authority from Rome, but in the governing and administering of their dioceses they were the Scottish king's tenants-in-chief and reported to him. In the thirteenth century the prelates' authority went beyond such formidable religious and administrative spheres for they also exercised a monopoly over education. Such princes of the church were the equal of other senior barons and the king consulted them on major issues affecting state security. As in England, it was younger sons who tended to make the church their career. Unlike their elder brothers, temporal lords and heirs to great estates that might well lie on both sides of the border, the bishops' allegiance tended to be firmly rooted in their Scottish dioceses and their native land.

Along with such native clergy the Scottish kings encouraged great monastic orders, such as the Benedictines and Augustinians, to settle in Scotland. From the thirteenth century onwards these were joined by mendicant orders – Dominicans, Franciscans and Carmelites. The first two in particular were given considerable wealth. Like the bishops the abbots of monasteries would have wide temporal responsibilities as well as religious ones. Their large and bounteous estates carried huge flocks of wool-producing sheep and they instituted other commercial undertakings. Such 'foreign' orders owed loyalty to the Scottish royal house and they tended to learn English before Gaelic. When teaching they used both English and Latin. The church represented a most powerful national force for three main reasons: its unceasing determination to be independent of Canterbury; due to its great concerns with the spiritual and material conditions of the Scottish people; and its large properties and commercial possessions, the gifts of successive Scottish kings.

If many distinctly Scottish institutions had been established or strengthened in the twelfth century they were undoubtedly developed in the years prior to Wallace's emergence. The years 1214 to 1286 have come to be seen as Scotland's early golden age. After thirty years of devastation, ending with the battle of Bannockburn in 1314, the chroniclers wrote that few old men could look back to that earlier time of peace and stability without deep longing. It was certainly a period when increasing numbers of people came to identify themselves with a Scottish state, a time when commerce thrived, and for some men the first occasion when their standard of living moved above subsistence level. Such material advances were not confined to great burghs such as Berwick, although that town became so successful its customs dues were reckoned at a quarter of all the English ports combined. The monks from Newbattle Abbey, near Dalkeith, sponsored additional industries, such as salt-making and even coal-mining, while traditional exports of hides and furs to both England and the Continent were joined by wool, livestock and fish. In Lothian an increasing number of high-born, English-speaking nobles with important interests south of the border were finding their possessions in the northern kingdom had grown more valuable still. Some of these would be likely to see future English policy towards Scotland reflecting envy at Scottish commercial success along with thoughts of royal domination.

Economic advances had also taken place on the land, still by far the main source of the country's wealth. The area put under the plough increased not only on the great estates but on the plots surrounding the expanding burghs and because of the increased numbers of smallholdings. It was only to be expected that whether great magnates or senior churchmen, burghers or husbandmen, they would bitterly resent any threats of increased tax demands, particularly if such officials acted for an English king.

Unsurprisingly, the Scottish church had benefited from the quickening of economic activity. As a result of the generosity of the Scottish kings and gifts from other wealthy penitents, together with the development of its estates and the exploitation of parish kirks, it had undertaken an ambitious building programme. This included an immense cathedral to Scotland's patron saint at St Andrews, the great transepts of Elgin and Dryburgh Abbeys, and the erection of Sweetheart Abbey, so-called because in 1273 it was bequeathed by Lady Dervorgilla Baliol for her husband, John. Any attempt by the English to anglicise the Scottish church or to treat it with any lack of respect would be sure to provoke determined opposition.

Particular resistance to English advances could be expected in another area, from among the nobility of the far north, that traditional focus of opposition to Scottish kings. By this time many of them had married into families of Anglo-Norman descent as well as native ones. In any case, there was no longer any alternative to the overlordship of the Scottish royal house and many nobles from the Highlands had come to watch its continuing respect for Celtic traditions with a degree of pride. Such proud, fierce men, who never shirked a fight, were likely to oppose English invaders and be well supported by kinsmen hardly less proud but equally quick to take affront.

Finally, in the south of Scotland there were people from relatively humble origins, the newly enfranchised and the relatively large number of minor lords whose perspectives tended to be circumscribed by local events, but whose loyalties to their country were fierce and strong. Both were accustomed to be educated by the minor clergy who in the thirteenth century were pious and fiercely patriotic.

William Wallace, the younger son of a Clydesdale laird, was educated in this way. At first he was taught by his uncle, who was parish priest at Dunipace, within the control of Cambuskenneth Abbey, near Stirling. Later he attended studies at Paisley Abbey. Tradition has it that when Wallace sat before his uncle at Dunipace he learned a passage which proved as important for him as the oath taken sixteen centuries before by the young Carthaginian, Hannibal, when he promised his father he would never be a friend to Rome. The words which Wallace committed to memory and apparently never tired of repeating were, 'Freedom is best, I tell thee true, of all things to be won. Then never live within the bond of slavery, my son.'[9]

Apart from the greater and lesser nobility, both lay and religious, in thirteenth-century Scotland there were other groups who had tasted freedom either by unshackling themselves from the burden of feudalism or by avoiding its yoke altogether, groups which could be expected to oppose and continue opposing the ambitions of an English king to bring their country, along with the rest of Britain, under his rule.

For all those men who were conscious of belonging to a single community of the realm of Scotland, whether proud Celt, or Norse earls from the Highlands, Norman knights with estates both north and south of the border, or freedom-loving, ordinary people who had never loved the Saxon, the end of the thirteenth century marked a time of both high challenge and great dangers.

CHAPTER TWO

≈

SCOTLAND'S
GREAT ADVERSARY

'Our remote situation hitherto, the retreat of freedom and on that account the more suspected, will
only serve to inflame the jealousy of our enemies.
We must therefore expect no mercy.'

Speech of Calgacus at Mons Graupius (AD 83)
Tacitus, Life of Agricola

IT WAS SCOTLAND'S ILL luck to suffer its worst constitutional
crisis for 250 years when England had a most formidable
and complex monarch. While Edward I was a self-proclaimed
champion of the chivalric code who could act with notable
generosity (generally when it suited his purpose), and who
marched to war with saintly banners overhead he was, too, a
Plantagenet, a sept of the Angevins who had a dire reputation
for evil. From relatively early in his life his reputation was
that of a man to be feared. Even before he became king a
contemporary English rhymer had likened him to a leopard,
considered at that time a devious animal. 'He is a lion by his
pride and ferocity, by his inconstancy and changeableness he
is a pard, changing his word and his promises, excusing himself
with fair speed.'[1]

Edward was tall and imposing, despite the drooping eyelid
inherited from his father, subtle-minded, with a strong seam
of cruelty in his character. The chronicler, Matthew Paris,
related how, before he became king, Edward caused another
young man whom he had never previously met to be taken
and mutilated while he was walking innocently down a road.
When king, Edward enlisted a small group of able men

– often outsiders – who were to serve him loyally. Among the Savoyards, for instance, were the long-serving Otto de Grandison and James of St George, the great castle-builder. Edward was careful never to raise any of his close associates to the rank of earl and although he could overlook corrupt practices when it suited him, he could also turn against men, however eminent, with frightening speed. An example here was his summary removal in 1295 of William March, his treasurer, and in 1302 of John Langton, his chancellor. To those considered disloyal Edward did not hesitate to implement the barbaric punishment of having them hung, drawn and quartered.

Edward was also extremely well versed in the law, which he was able to interpret to his own advantage. Surprisingly self-confident, even as a young man, he was a brave, indefatigable soldier and unquestionably a great statesman-king of his time. His biographer, Michael Prestwich, acknowledged his single-minded approach: 'A hard-headed ruler determined to uphold his rights as he saw them, and ruthless in the methods he adopted to achieve his ends. There was for him no inconsistency between his pursuit of such ideals on the crusade and the determined practicality of the way he ruled in England.'[2]

What more important aim could there possibly be for such an English monarch than the enlargement of his home country, initially through diplomatic means and, if this failed, by military action?

Some indication of Edward's methods, and what he probably had in store for Scotland, can be gathered from his actions in Wales, the subjection of which (apart from the defence of important English interests in France and his zeal for crusading) was to become his main objective between 1276 and 1284. In 1277, at the end of the first Welsh wars, Edward downgraded the political authority of the greatest of the Welsh princes, Llywelyn. Although he subsequently exercised mercy by releasing Llywelyn from a huge indemnity and sponsored his marriage to Eleanor de Montfort, this only served to bind the Welshman more closely to English court circles. Edward moved steadily forward with the reduction of Wales, using a combination of legal and military means, blocking Welsh powers of jurisdiction and building a line of strong castles across the country. Hardly surprisingly, rather than lose all their remaining powers, the Welsh princes – in both the north and south of the country – rose against him a second time. In the ensuing conflict Llywelyn was killed and Prince Dafyd, his brother was captured and made to suffer the terrible punishments which Edward had devised for traitors. From now onwards he proceeded with a programme of entirely suppressing the country. After the English system of administration had been extended, the English-style counties of Flint, Anglesey, Merioneth and Caernarvon were created and the country was firmly controlled by English Lords marcher faithful to Edward. The Statute of Wales, issued on 19 March 1284, began by explaining how Wales, feudally dependent on England, was now 'wholly and entirely transferred under our proper dominion', united and annexed to England. Welsh laws and customs had been duly considered and some were to continue, while others were corrected or added to. The king appealed to divine providence as justifying his actions.[3]

The process of castle-building was extended to include a magnificent royal one at Caernarvon. In the classic fashion, along with the castles came new towns, within which Edward pushed forward the economic and social conversion of the country. As the English medieval scholar T.F. Tout put it, the intention of such military and civil administration 'was to teach civility to the wild Welsh by the stimulating example of the English soldiers, traders and clergy whose business was to direct them, not necessarily too gently in the right way.'[4]

In the towns of Edward's brave new Wales Welshmen were not allowed to apply for burgesses' posts – these were reserved for good Englishmen – and Jews, with whom the Welsh had previously enjoyed a working relationship, were stopped from taking active roles there.

In the autumn of 1294, as the king was preparing to leave for Gascony to fight the French, the Welsh, led by Madog ap Llywelyn, rose in revolt for a final time. On this occasion many ordinary citizens were involved, and their numbers were increased by a proportion of the Welsh soldiers whom Edward had recruited into the English army and who now refused to serve overseas. As much as anything else it was this calling up of Welsh contingents for France which set Wales ablaze with resentment. Edward's response was quick and efficient and the Welsh proved no military match for English cavalry supported by archers. By July 1295 the king was able to make a triumphant tour of the principality which, as an independent country, had ceased to exist. His object achieved, Edward now graciously agreed to investigate and remedy the alleged abuses committed by his tax officials, apparently a powerful factor towards popular support of the rebellion.

This was the calibre of the English king who, by decree and conquest, eliminated the Welsh state. Scotland, with its unbroken line of kings and different history, might be a dissimilar case. But once determined to enlarge his authority in that kingdom, clear-sighted Scots should have had few illusions about their likely fate at the hands of such a man – unless they could mount more effective opposition on both a national and even an international scale.

In an age when a strong monarch was of paramount importance, Scotland's fortunes changed radically for the worse with the sudden and untimely death, at the age of forty-four, of King Alexander III. On a dark, snow-laden night in March 1286, he hastened to join his new wife at Kinghorn in Fife beside the Firth of Forth. At some stage of the journey, after outdistancing his outriders, his horse lost its footing and threw him on the rocky foreshore. This gave his brother-in-law, the English king, a notable chance to intervene in Scottish affairs, as in the past Scottish kings had done when dynastic quarrels occurred south of the border. With Edward, though, his ambition was greater and his determination became absolute. Although Edward had been thwarted in his aim to become the arbiter of Europe, by 1286 the conquest of Wales was well advanced. That such a strong and aspiring king, highly skilled in both constitutional procedures and legal matters, should ignore an opportunity for extending English power north of the border was not to be imagined. Whether or not he set out consciously in 1286 to subdue a state which had been for so long an independent kingdom, during the later years of his life it became his consuming aim. Even in his final campaign, when he was close to death and his mind had started to wander, he still pledged himself 'before God and the swans to overwhelm Scotland once and for all'. (The swans referred to were likely to have been the roasted and decorated birds which, in 1307, were given pride of place on the royal table during celebrations for another military conquest, and the appointment of his son as Prince of Wales.)

Strictly speaking it was not Alexander's death that gave the English king his opportunity. This came about because Alexander's successor to the throne of Scotland was his sickly three-year-old grandchild, Margaret of Norway (daughter of Eric II of Norway and his Scottish wife Margaret, who died giving birth to her). King Alexander was fully aware of the likely dangers to the state in the event of his death and had already taken the precaution of making his subjects recognise his grand-daughter as his heir, providing, of course, no other children were born to him. In fact, prior to the enthronement of the infant Margaret, it was arranged that the government of Scotland should be placed in the custody of six men appointed to act as Guardians of the Kingdom. Two of the six were bishops, William Fraser of St Andrews and Robert Wishart of Glasgow; two earls, Duncan of Fife and Alexander Comyn of Buchan; and two barons, John Comyn of Badenoch and James the Steward. The two most likely contenders for the throne in the event of the princess's death, Robert Bruce (the Competitor) and John Baliol, were not invited to act as Guardians although each had his supporters amongst the six.

One of the Guardians' first acts was to send a delegation to Edward, as king of England and lord superior to so many of the Scottish nobility. This informed him as a matter of courtesy about the arrangements being made for governing Scotland in the absence of the maid, Margaret. Edward's response was to express sympathy and apparent approval for their actions to preserve an independent Scotland.

Some writers maintain that had Edward always been determined to conquer Scotland, he would surely have taken advantage of the great opportunity which occurred in the early years of the interregnum. In reality it was far more complicated than they suggest, given Edward's difficulties, for instance, with France over Gascony. It is not clear who originated the scheme for a marriage between his son Edward, Prince of Wales, and the infant Margaret but he was active in promoting it and sent an emissary to Norway in April 1290. It certainly offered him considerable scope. If it went ahead he could work towards an 'incorporating union' of both countries under the English crown. If it came to nothing – and the king's spies would scarcely have neglected telling him how sickly the little princess was – he would still be able to appear both majestic and statesmanlike while retaining his close involvement in Scottish affairs. Edward's agreement was formally accepted by the Scots during August 1290 through the treaty of Birgham, in which he acknowledged that Scotland would remain free and independent, save for the right of the English king relating 'to matters concerning the Marches or elsewhere before the time of the present concession'.[5] Before the treaty was signed he had already exercised his rights under this clause by taking the Isle of Man under his protection claiming that the earl of Ulster had surrendered it to him and ignoring strong Scottish claims. He also appointed Anthony Bec, bishop of Durham, to administer justice and set the realm in order, requiring all Scottish fortifications to be placed in his hands (in order to prevent internal unrest before the accession of a new monarch). With the Maid's death in September 1290, the treaty of Birgham came to nothing.

With twelve possible claimants for the vacant throne, as well as Eric of Norway, Scotland obviously faced a serious succession crisis, although the two principal candidates were John Baliol and Robert Bruce (see table of The Scottish Succession on p. vi).

At this point one of the Guardians, Bishop William Fraser, who was well disposed towards the English king, wrote informing him that Robert Bruce had made his play for the crown by going to Perth with a great following. In view of this, Fraser formally requested Edward to adjudicate over the succession process to avoid civil bloodshed. At the same time he made it clear he favoured Baliol. The second cleric acting as a Guardian, Bishop Wishart, together with the baron James the Steward, both favoured Bruce, but given the virtual certainty of internal conflict without an arbiter acceptable to both sides, they also agreed to accept Edward's ruling. Edward graciously undertook the task and, having gathered the feudal army of north England around him to support his authority, summoned the Scottish nobles and clergy to leave their own country and come to meet him at Norham, near Berwick. There he told them he could judge their various claims to the throne only if he was regarded as Lord Paramount of Scotland. There seemed little opportunity to object at this stage, and at Upsettlington on the Tweed eight of the claimants – joined rapidly by John Baliol – formally acknowledged Edward as their Lord Superior.

The full extent of the English king's ambitions towards Scotland now became evident when during 1291 in a statement made to his privy council he told them 'that he had it in his mind to bring under his dominion the king and the realm of Scotland'.[6]

After the Scots accepted Edward as arbitrator there followed what has been called the 'splendid façade' – the time spent by him in leisurely judgement. On 11 June 1291 the English king ordered all Scottish castles to be turned over to him until two months after he had decided on the succession, and he replaced many Scottish officials by Englishmen. As Edward made a formal progression to Perth everyone was required to pay homage or to be kept under arrest until they did. It was not until eighteen months later on 17 November 1292 that Edward declared Baliol to be the rightful heir by reason of both English and Scottish law, although he qualified the award with the sinister reservation 'saving our right and that of our heirs when we shall wish to speak thereupon'.[7] The debate on the succession aroused complex and technical arguments and Edward, the upholder of the law, took great pains over how the pleading was conducted. A court was set up containing 104 auditors, forty nominated by both Baliol and Bruce and twenty-four by Edward himself. Initially discussion took place over which law should be followed – feudal law favoured Baliol, Roman law Bruce – and then whether Scotland could be divided between daughters and their descendants. Nothing was hurried and one adjournment lasted from August 1291 until June 1292 to enable the Count of Holland (one of the lesser candidates) to fetch a document vital for his case. Eventually the verdict went to Baliol: latter-day historians are agreed about his case appearing the strongest in law.

In late November, after swearing an oath of allegiance to his Lord Superior, Baliol was enthroned at Scone like other Scottish kings before him. As Edward no doubt anticipated, Baliol quickly revealed certain weaknesses of character. In any case he had probably been intended for the church and lacked training in politics and war. He experienced difficulties from the outset. A burgess from Berwick appealed to Edward against judgements given in the court of the Guardians, Scotland's highest court during the interregnum. It appeared to be a deliberate test case. The English king's reply must have devastated Baliol. Edward contended that in his feudal capacity he had the right to hear whatever appeals might be made and, even more serious, to summon the king of Scotland to appear before him. Baliol found himself required to make arduous journeys to London and, once there, to defend the judgements of his own courts. Edward's intensification of his overlordship reached its climax when he appeared to treat the Scottish state as part of his feudal property by summoning both the Scottish king and certain of his lords to serve on his coming military campaign in France and by levying taxes on Scotland for it. When Baliol reported this to his council at Scone they were enraged and, by taking charge of affairs of state themselves, acknowledged the terrible dangers that beset their country.

Because of the difficulties which Edward experienced in collecting an army for overseas service – including the serious reservations raised by many of his English nobles – the Scots' response could hardly have come as a surprise to him. In their anger the Scots turned towards France as a possible ally and, after declaring all English nobles' lands in Scotland to be forfeit, expelled such landed proprietors from the northern kingdom. Edward thereupon postponed his expedition to France, for his first priority lay in dealing with the defiant Scots together with the Welsh who were also in revolt. After the Welsh were subdued – as it turned out forever – his full wrath fell upon Scotland, and on 1 March 1296 he joined the army which he had assembled at Newcastle-upon-Tyne prior to its movement north.

Meanwhile on Easter Monday the Scottish feudal host (with some notable absentees, including Robert Bruce) had already taken the military initiative, and moved south across the English border. Unable to take the strong fortress of Carlisle the Scots had to content themselves with ravaging the adjoining countryside. Over the next month they remained in Northumberland, where they burned religious houses and killed many defenceless people.

While the foray showed the Scots possessed the will and the capacity to oppose English domination, it was markedly unsuccessful as a military operation. The English response was far more effective. Edward selected the great trading centre of Berwick as his quarry and, after piercing its modest defences, he allowed his troops thirty-six hours of pillage and butchery. As it had refused to yield, the contemporary conventions of warfare gave him the right to act in this way, and he might have reasoned – correctly as it turned out – that after such an example other Scottish burghs would not dare similar defiance, but the savage methods he adopted shocked and angered Scots of all classes. In this sense it proved counter-productive, helping to fuel their patriotic feelings and confirming their hatred rather than apprehension and dislike of the English. Berwick was never to regain its former prominence and although Edward, in seeming regret, offered to help rebuild it and, in 1302, actually made it a free burgh, he took pains to resettle it with Englishmen. The result was its detachment from Scotland although its formal inclusion into England did not occur, of course, until modern times. The parallel of his action here with his methods in Wales was surely an indication of his plans for the whole of Scotland.

Following Berwick the English, led by John Warenne, earl of Surrey, moved further into Scotland meeting the Scots in battle at Dunbar. The engagement occurred there as a result of contrasting loyalties among the Dunbar family. While Patrick, earl of Dunbar, was loyal to Edward, his wife turned to the Scottish cause and succeeded in admitting a Scottish force into Dunbar Castle. On hearing this Edward ordered a cavalry division under Warenne to recapture it.

On 27 April 1296, the English knights who were besieging the castle found themselves about to be attacked by Baliol who had arrived with his main army, the Scottish feudal host. Warenne's response was well judged. He kept some detachments before the castle walls to prevent the Scottish garrison emerging and joining up with their compatriots. Leaving these forces under the command of his junior officers he moved with his veteran horsemen to meet the main Scottish army as it came over the brow of Spottsmuir Hill. In doing so, the English had to cross a steep valley with the Spott Burn at its base. As they made their best way across it they broke formation and some units temporarily disappeared from the Scots line of sight. With fatal presumption the Scots assumed the English were in flight. They were, of course, quite mistaken, but with their horses they left their strong defensive positions on the hilltop and rushed headlong down its slopes in pursuit. As their horses varied in strength and quality and some took more direct routes than others they met with their opponents in penny packets. In any case, aware of what was happening the English had ample time to form up before the Scots were upon them. The result was inevitable. The Scots cavalry was quickly sent flying back across Lammermuir from where it sought the shelter of Selkirk Forest some forty miles to the west. Meanwhile, the English cavalry turned at its leisure against the Scottish foot and inflicted heavy casualties upon them to give Surrey a complete victory.

So ended the battle of Dunbar where the Scots showed lack of military astuteness. Admittedly there was some excuse: with the exception of the limited engagement against the Norse at the battle of Largs they had experienced no serious fighting since Alexander II's campaign in Galloway during 1235. Recent inexperience, though, could hardly justify such arrogance and fatal overconfidence. There had been no need to risk their mounted forces against Warenne's experienced cavalry and in the case of a reverse to allow their infantry to be ridden down. Equally serious, they made no attempt to draw the English on into inhospitable country as another Scottish leader would do soon afterwards. Many highborn Scots were captured during the cavalry engagement and found themselves in English prisons far from their kinsmen north of the border.

Following Dunbar Edward proceeded to make a triumphal progress through the country, leaving men in little doubt about his intentions for full conquest when he ordered the sacred relics of Scotland, the symbolic Stone of Destiny (upon which all past Scottish kings had been enthroned) to be carried off to Westminster Abbey, along with the Black Rood of St Margaret, wife of Malcolm III. He also filled carts with three chests of the royal records together with as much plate as he could find. These were sent rumbling southwards and their contents have never been seen since.

On 10 July 1296 John Baliol, stripped of his robes and carrying the rod of a penitent, was forced to surrender his kingdom and enter into captivity. At a parliament held in Berwick during August Edward unveiled his plan for the country's subjugation, which began with his decree that all substantial landowners should give or renew their oath of fealty to him as Lord of Scotland. Almost 1500 men, including the clergy, signed what came to be known as the 'Ragman Roll'. Among the names was that of Robert Bruce who, by refusing to answer the Scottish feudal summons raised by Baliol, had his estate of Annandale placed under the earl of Buchan. The English king now had it returned to him. Edward appointed English officials to govern the country under his direct representative, Warenne, earl of Surrey, who was assisted by Hugh Cressingham as treasurer, Walter Amersham as chancellor and William Ormsby as justiciar. All subsidiary posts were also filled by English officials.

Ten years after Alexander III's death it seemed as if Scotland was sharing a similar fate as Wales and no medieval soothsayer would have given much hope for its future independence unless a new leader could be found or, as a far from young man, Edward might die before his work had become irreversible.

The qualities needed to meet this mortal threat to Scotland's continued existence were hardly ordinary ones. For the Scots the time for diplomacy had long passed; military measures were the only hope although, after Dunbar, their chances of success here appeared minimal. Fortunately for them – some would say miraculously – they possessed a leader who, seemingly against all odds, was able to tilt the balance in their favour.

CHAPTER THREE

≈

WALLACE RAISES HIS HEAD

'In the year 1297 that distinguished warrior
William Wallace, the hammer and scourge of
the English, the son of an illustrious Knight of the
same name began to act a conspicuous part.'

John of Fordun

IN SEPTEMBER 1296, AS the English king set out on his
delayed journey to France, he had reason to feel well
pleased at the success of his campaign to control Scotland.
Although he already chose to view it as a northward extension
of England rather than a separate kingdom, he might still have
felt a measure of surprise that such a rugged country with its
fiercely independent, proud people had apparently submitted
more easily than Wales. Admittedly the Scottish military forces
had shown themselves remarkably inept and the nobility had
quickly been made to swear fealty to him, although he was fully
aware they did so with markedly different levels of enthusiasm.
But did he not hold many of their near and dear in England to
guarantee their good behaviour? And was he not taking others
to France to prove their loyalty? Their last pathetic king had
been humiliated and was he not securely held in England?

As for the Bruces, the other main candidates for the Scottish
throne, had not old Robert Bruce 'the Competitor' died in 1295
and his son declared his friendship with Edward? Admittedly
this was in the hope of being considered for the vacant
throne, but he was now being made to prove his loyalty as
commander of Carlisle garrison – the first objective of any
Scottish military expedition southward – while his twenty-two-
year-old son had quietly gone back to his own estates. Did

Edward's representatives not hold all the many offices of state both high and low, while English soldiers garrisoned the Scottish castles? Bolstered by such thoughts the English king's confidence must have been increased further with his poor opinion of the Scots, which he revealed in a remark to his controller, Surrey, as he was about to leave for the Continent. They had been discussing future tactics and the king, who in all likelihood thought he was recommending what would turn out as a final solution for Scotland, ended the exchange with the caustic words, 'He does good business who rids himself of a turd.'[1]

As in Wales prior to 1295, it was unthinkable that all opposition had ended so tamely, although it was still difficult to imagine where the source of trouble would be. Edward was fond of making bets with his household staff and if wagers had been struck about the region most likely to rebel, the Highlands would surely have warranted the shortest odds. With the exception of Galloway, English control over southern Scotland seemed far more complete. To confound such thinking, within a year serious resistance had occurred in both the north and south of the country, with equally menacing effects.

Edward's very contempt for the Scots was partly to blame here for, while he had browbeaten the Scottish magnates into supporting him, he gave them nothing like the rewards offered to the Welsh Lords marcher. Given his unwillingness to treat them generously and the deep regard which many felt for their native or even their adopted country, he should have been wary about their continuing support. Furthermore he had alienated many of the common people by choosing to appoint English officials both to uphold his authority and collect his revenues, men who themselves shared his scorn of the Scots. Shrewd as he was, he also failed to appreciate the hatred he was bound to arouse in the Scottish church when he decided to substitute English for Scottish clergy.

While history shows that effective opposition to oppressive regimes relies on men who are prepared to hazard their lives and whose chances of success depend heavily upon their military skills, such men need much help from others. While no doubt less bold physically, influential men must show themselves willing to accept responsibility for orchestrating the liberation movement countrywide. The Scottish church was soon to play this vital role against the English.

Despite such powerful factions, if the general climate of dissent remains lukewarm, freedom fighters can never hope to recruit successfully. To legitimise their deeds they need to have a good measure of popular support, too. In essence, there has to be a strong sense of national identity. Scottish historians, including Geoffrey Barrow, feel that within Scotland of the thirteenth century, there was already some sense of collective entity although one wonders whether this could be termed nationalism in its more modern sense. It cannot be denied, however, that by 1297, when William Wallace and Andrew Moray raised their respective standards in both the south and north of the country, there was a burning spirit of resentment and unrest across the land against English domination, with both influential and lesser figures supporting the rebellion.

The English chronicler, Hemingburgh, and the monks who contributed to the Lanercost Chronicle, were certain the revolt was both instigated and co-ordinated by two of the Guardians during the interregnum, the cleric Robert Wishart, bishop of Glasgow, and the baron, James the Steward, Wallace's feudal superior. The Lanercost chronicle described in angry terms about both men and the Scottish church in general:

'For with one accord both those who discharged the office of prelate and those who were preachers, corrupted the ears and minds of nobles and commons, by advice and exhortation, both publicly and secretly, stirring them to enmity against that King and nation who had so effectively delivered them.'
'. . . For the bishop of the Church in Glasgow whose personal name was Robert Wishart, ever foremost in treason, conspirant with the Steward of the realm named James, for a new piece of insolence, yea, for a new chapter of ruin. Not daring openly to break their pledged faith to the King, they counsel a certain

bloody man, William Wallace, who had been chief of brigands in Scotland, to revolt against the King and assemble the people in his support.'[2]

While both Wallace and Moray were loyal sons of the church, commentators have been divided about the extent of the direct influence and control which the church had over them. The Highland writer Evan Barron, for instance, did not see Bishop Wishart's hand behind their separate risings during the winter of 1296 but recognised him as the instigator and organiser of the more general revolt in the spring of 1297. There is no consensus today. Of the recent writers on Wallace, Andrew Fisher and James Mackay consider both Wallace and Moray led their own men, followed their own impulses and took their own risks, with Wishart and the Steward co-ordinating rather than inciting their activities; while D.J. Gray sees Wishart behind their every move.

Whatever the exact nature of the relations between the young fighting men and their backers, it was fortunate for Scotland that they both enjoyed support from many quarters. As for historical acclaim, while Wallace captured popular sympathy both during his lifetime and down the succeeding years, Andrew Moray was virtually forgotten until the beginning of the twentieth century. Then Evan Barron attempted to reinstate him and put him forward as 'one of the chivalric figures of Scottish history and in all likelihood before his untimely death a greater soldier than Wallace'.[3] While this latter assertion is hardly proven, despite its special pleading, Barron's scholarly and vigorous account has helped to vindicate Moray's part in the struggle against the English and show the support he could mobilise.

Son of Sir Andrew Moray of Petty, he came from one of the great Highland families and together with his father and uncle was present at Dunbar. All three were taken prisoner there and confined at Chester but Andrew escaped – possibly through help organised by Bishop Wishart – and made his way back to the family lands in the far north.

Barron's story of Andrew Moray's arrival at the family stronghold adjoining Avoch on the Black Isle (north of Inverness), the raising of his standard there, and the coming together of small bodies of men loyal to the Moray family, both vassals and tenants, along with citizens from Inverness led by an eager burgess, Alexander Pilche, is the stuff of Highland legend. The young man and his followers were able to use their knowledge of the ground to compensate for the much superior equipment of the English, especially their armoured knights. Andrew Moray's skills were revealed in his successful ambush of Sir William Fitzwarine, the constable of Urquhart Castle. Shortly afterwards, through various ruses combined with brave deeds, a steady stream of northern castles – including the key one of Inverness – began to fall into the hands of his growing band.

Responding to the dangers posed by Moray, Edward had two Scottish lords, John Comyn of Badenoch and John Comyn, earl of Buchan, released from their service in France and charged to help deal with him. Both Comyns, with some claims to the Scottish throne themselves, failed to act as Edward hoped and Edward's treasurer, Cressingham, strongly suspected them of being less than loyal to the English king. In any event Moray not only survived but was so successful that, by July 1297, the English contingents in the north east were compelled to emerge from their castle strongholds and take the field against him. Shorn of its garrisons the whole region rose in revolt and the critical castle of Aberdeen fell to the Scots. Moray now found himself free to join forces with another young but outstanding leader for a major military engagement further south. It is generally agreed that William Wallace was a younger son of Sir Malcolm Wallace of Elderslie near Paisley, and that his mother was daughter of Sir Reginald Crawford of Crosbie, hereditary sheriff of Ayr. Despite this much humbler, if still respectable, background he is far better known than Andrew Moray and infinitely better known than other leading Scottish patriots of the time. In Moray's case his premature death ended a career which might just possibly have surpassed Wallace's own, but the others never achieved the same military successes and therefore never merited such fame. It is true that Wallace enjoyed the advantage of his dauntless publicist, Henry the Rhymer (Blind Harry), although this is, of course, far from the whole story. Harry's rambling adulatory and unashamedly populist work brings its problems, too, but it is our only source for certain stages of Wallace's life. It certainly succeeds in stirring our emotions and, whatever his reasons, its author leaves us in no doubt that, during his lifetime and beyond, Wallace represented an immensely powerful symbol for Scottish independence. However, by the time of Wallace's death, almost 200 years before Harry's account, his military deeds alone were notable enough to merit the highest acclaim.

Before turning to such deeds it helps to have some picture of him as a man. The one contemporary source, the sympathetic Scottish chronicler, John of Fordun, gives the shortest of descriptions about Wallace's personal qualities, describing him as 'wondrously brave and bold, of goodly mien and boundless liberality'. Fortunately there is other evidence that allows us to go some way further.

Physically, while not as tall as King Edward, Wallace was exceptionally strong. No short man, for instance, could have carried – and used to such startlingly good effect – a sword fully 5ft 7in long. He was much younger than the English king, and uncommonly young to hold high military command, a fact corroborated by the description of him at his first great battle as a juvenis (a young man). It has been reckoned that Wallace was born on or about the same time as Robert Bruce, later King, which would have made him twenty-five years of age when he, with Moray as his lieutenant, commanded the Scottish forces at Stirling. His youth has puzzled successive biographers. How, they ask, could he emerge with such fully developed military skills? Andrew Fisher, for example, has put forward the possibility that Wallace might already have served in an English army. If he did serve with the English it seems almost unthinkable that no mention was made of it by Blind Harry or one of the other chroniclers of the time. In any case, William Wallace was hardly the first young man to gain notable military successes. Alexander the Great had conquered the known world by the time he was thirty-one, while Hannibal became commander-in-chief of the Phoenician forces at the age of twenty-six. But for want of other evidence, we are brought back to the traditional approach taken by Blind Harry that Wallace learned his military trade as an outlaw. As a fugitive he would certainly have become accustomed to meeting grave dangers. He would have also learned how to use ground effectively and come to understand the importance of timing, speed of movement and deception. He must have recognised, too, the need for his companions to understand his methods of fighting and to remain sanguine when undertaking operations against superior numbers.

Like the young Hannibal we can be sure that Wallace would have been able to withstand the cold and hardships of military life. Anyone who based himself in the Forest of Selkirk during his early campaigns and later used the woods as a haven for months and years at a time had to be physically robust and capable of ignoring personal discomforts. In his early campaigns, once his particular military object had been achieved, like all great guerrilla leaders Wallace would melt back into the sheltering forest.

The portrait of Wallace held by Paisley Central Library, and the frontispiece of this book, shows him in classic pose, wearing a fantastical protective helmet. Beneath the headwear is a young – if not very young – face which while not strikingly handsome has a wide forehead, large reflective eyes and an impressive jaw. There is a calmness and quiet confidence about the subject which is difficult to reconcile with a mindless avenger or a man blind to the wants of others.

Whatever Wallace's personal appearance, Fordun is quite clear about his bravery and boldness. It is no surprise to find that both qualities were emphasised by Blind Harry in his description of Wallace's many personal encounters. We can be sure, though, that Harry was following the accepted tradition relating to his hero. Wallace's whole life demonstrated his boldness. Swift to act, brilliant in minor and then grand stratagems, fully prepared to adopt novel military formations, he had the nerve to take on the might of England's military power. Despite his youth, junior rank and inexperience, he was willing to assume the sole direction of Scotland's military and political affairs at a time of the gravest national crisis.

Fordun's reference to Wallace's boundless liberality is the quality most difficult to endorse. One feels bound to wonder whether there was not an element of sycophancy here, for Wallace was in many ways a frightening man. Yet we have contemporary evidence of his determination to spare women, children and priests from his bloody soldiery. Equally telling was his ability to lead ordinary men into situations of utmost danger where the odds were highly unfavourable. Those who joined him, whether nobles or ordinary men, showed themselves willing to die on his behalf. Wallace's own liberality can possibly best be seen in his willingness to sacrifice everything for his country.

The quality which Fordun did not seize upon in his epigrammatic description was Wallace's sense of mission, although his reference to Wallace's boldness approached it. Wallace lived in an age when men frequently broke their most solemn pledges – without any sense of guilt if they thought they had made them under duress – and when despite the religious tenor of the time, deceit and subterfuge were the currency of most other prominent figures in both England and Scotland. He was incapable of making terms with an English king (if we can believe Edward's offer of leniency to him). For Wallace saw him as nothing more than a royal freebooter: a man who would ruthlessly use the privileges of his great office, his regal status with holy church, his power of feudal patronage, and even bribes from his exchequer to suborn those who tried to uphold the independence of Scotland.

Such commitment helps to explain Wallace's own implacability, his pitilessness in his treatment of English oppressors and traitors. The English chroniclers recognised the enmity of this unyielding man from Welsh Norman stock by likening him to a bogeyman. They were surely right, for his determination to defeat the English forces, together with his limitless pride in his native country, seemingly made him incapable of trimming his sails to fortune like other of his more exalted contemporaries. Even in his darkest hour he still had the pride and dignity to deny he could ever be called a traitor, on the grounds that he had never sworn allegiance to the English king. This was surely more than the lack of imagination which Geoffrey Barrow points to as one of his character defects. The pride shown by Shakespeare's Roman hero, Coriolanus, might be closer to the mark, although Wallace's attempts to spare women and children and his strong Christian beliefs leavened Coriolanus' Roman sense of fatalism.

Hated as he was by the English, Wallace, like Coriolanus, did not lack opponents among his own people either. The indomitable nature of one who demanded so much of others lacking his degree of patriotism – nobly born and ordinary men alike – who then rode roughshod over them if they were reluctant or demurred, repelled many.

From Blind Harry's account of Wallace's early military exploits, prior to the spring of 1297 the possibility of Wallace being betrayed by one or more of his compatriots seemed remote. From the beginning Harry the Rhymer's account stressed both Wallace's maturity and apparent disregard for superior numbers. His aim of terrorising English officials in Scotland led him to attack Selby, the son of Dundee's English constable. Despite Wallace being alone and Selby's ample bodyguard – "Yet, for all his men that sembled him about" – Harry tells us that Wallace's sword got through and Selby was killed. Wallace is closely pursued by Selby's followers and we are told of his being helped by a good wife who dressed him up as a young girl and set him before a spinning wheel. When the English dashed into the house they naturally failed to see through the disguise!

> In that same house they sought him busily,
> But he sat still and spun right cunningly.

It is tempting to dismiss Harry's hackneyed description of his escape out of hand until one remembers that, on his escape to Skye, Prince Charles Edward dressed as Flora MacDonald's serving maid. If factually accurate Harry's words support Wallace's youthful appearance, 'Sad of countenance he was both old and young'.

The Rhymer then describes a number of incidents by which he can demonstrate Wallace's continuing disregard for danger and unyielding enmity for the English. Eventually, even Wallace can cheat the odds no longer and he is taken and flung into prison. Harry is aghast for who else has his courage and resolution?

> Living as now a Chieftan have we none
> Durst take on hand but young Wallace alone
> This land is lost. He caught is in the snare.

There follows a remarkable episode where the English give up his body for dead but he is nursed back to life by the daughter of his old nurse. Anyone doubting the allegorical nature of Harry's Wallace and feeling tempted to treat the poem as a strictly factual account should read this section carefully. The reality was more likely to have been the bribing of gaolers combined with exaggerated reports of his illness.

After Wallace's recovery Harry has him involved in larger engagements with a growing number of followers. At Loudoun Hill near Irvine, for instance, they ambushed an English convoy, killing or wounding 100 men, and seized all its supplies. Harry condones Wallace's savagery here by explaining that it was an act of revenge for the execution of his father and brother, a fact which remains uncertain. In this engagement Harry describes the outstanding use which Wallace and his companions make of their swords, 'on foot great room about them made'.

Other combats followed and we have Wallace entering into a liaison with a girl who confessed she had betrayed him; he magnanimously spares her life before making good his escape from her apartment, again using the device of dressing in her clothes! Together with other military initiatives – always on an ascending scale – Harry recounts how Wallace married a Marion Braidfoot who lived in Lanark and reported the birth of a child 'Which goodly was, a maiden bright and sheen'.

Wallace's respect for churches and members of the clergy is supported by other accounts, but Harry alone relates the occasion when the English attempted to capture both Wallace and his loyal companion, Sir John Graham, while they were at worship (and therefore unarmed). Both fled to Marion's home and rushing through it escaped over the Cartland Crags behind. Harry describes how Marion was killed as she tried to delay their pursuers who then burnt her house.

> Put her to death I cannot tell you how
> Of like matter I may not tarry now.

That night he has a vengeful Wallace slaying William Heselrig, the English appointee as Sheriff of Lanark, and his son before putting their house to the torch. Harry even has him hacking Heselrig's body into pieces. For Harry that was not the end of the affray; another of Wallace's men killed Heselrig's deputy and, according to the Rhymer, a further twelvescore Englishmen died although 'women they left and priests upon the morn'. We know for certain that Wallace slew Heselrig although there is only Harry's word that he did it to avenge his wife and he hacked the body into pieces. Considering Wallace's later conduct there can be no doubt about his capacity to do so, but the incident fits almost too neatly into the picture Harry draws of a grief-stricken, wronged and vengeful young hero striking against his English oppressors.

By contrast, the chronicler John of Fordun emphasises the military significance of Heselrig's death in line with Wallace's earlier killing of Selby. When, in Fordun's words, Wallace first 'lifted up his head from his den' in May 1297 and emerged from the cover of the forest of Selkirk to murder William Heselrig he declared his intent.[4] From now onwards no English official in the south could feel secure against the avenging Scots. Andrew Moray's northern insurrection – where they were already killing or confining the king's officers – was now counterbalanced by a new insurgent leader.

Andrew Fisher puts forward the less romantic possibility that Wallace might have had other personal reasons for murdering Heselrig, namely that as neither he nor his brother had been recorded as pledging their loyalty to the English king they may have already been outlawed or punished in some other fashion. Whatever the motives the effect was the same, to terrorise English officials. The act was also the signal for a general uprising.[5]

Blind Harry provides much seemingly authentic detail about the relatively few nobles willing to place themselves under Wallace's banner, including some who already had relatives serving with him and others not yet ready to make a formal commitment:

> Sir Ranneld then sent him his power haill
> Himself durst not be know in battail
> Against Southeron for he had made a band
> Long time ago before to hold of them his land
> Adam Wallace past out of Richardtown
> And Robert Boyd with good men of renown
> Of Cunningham and Kyle came men of Haill
> ... Three thousand haill of likely men in wear
> And fed on foot which wanted horse and gear.

The poet went further than any other commentator, describing them as seeking leadership from a young man whose happiness had been blighted for ever by his loss of a wife and other dearest kin. Harry placed Wallace in a situation analagous to that of Field Marshal Montgomery who, six and a half centuries later, after losing his wife in tragic circumstances concentrated exclusively on war.

> Now leave thy youth now follow thy hard chance
> Now leave thy lust now leave thy marriage
> Now leave thy love or thou shalt lose a gage
> Which never in earth shall be redeemed again
> Follow fortune and all her fierce outrage
> Go live in war, go live in cruel pain.

From now onwards Wallace, whether he was grieving or not for his Marion, commanded something resembling an army rather than a comparatively small band of loyal and desperate men. He now enjoyed further military successes and failed only narrowly to assassinate the largest of quarries, Edward's justiciar in Scotland, William Ormsby. For this operation he was joined by another courageous fighter, Sir William Douglas, who had been forced to surrender Berwick Castle to Edward during the previous year. Wallace's forces lay near Lanark and Ormsby's official residence at Scone was over eighty miles away. It is likely that Wallace made a raid on it with a relatively small mounted force of well-trained soldiers. Unfortunately for them, agents alerted Ormsby of their approach and he escaped in the nick of time – although he was forced to leave his valuables behind.

The twin campaigns of Moray in the north and Wallace in the south put the English temporarily on the defensive and inspired other Scots to chance their arm. Men of higher office than the two young insurgents, including some who favoured the Bruce faction, such as Bishop Wishart, James the Steward, young Robert Bruce himself together with Douglas (who left Wallace to join them), came out in a separate rebellion. The English moved rapidly against it and on 7 July 1297 at Irvine they brought up superior forces and the Scots, hampered by internal wrangling, cravenly surrendered without a fight.

Wallace meanwhile had shown a different level of determination together with a marked degree of ruthlessness against friends and enemies alike, and after the disgrace at Irvine he emerged as a leader in his own right beyond any earlier position he might have held as the agent of James the Steward and Bishop Wishart. This was seen in his anger at Wishart's weak showing at Irvine – despite his valuable support in many other ways. Wallace apparently raided his palace and took away some of his possessions, even taking his sons.[6] Ever in Wallace's mind at this time was the need for a major battle where the Scots must acquit themselves better than at Dunbar or Irvine. Even as he continued to mount successful local actions, he kept his main forces based on the forest of Selkirk and concentrated on augmenting his strength there while drilling them in new tactics more appropriate for an army formation. Wallace now ordered other Scottish nobles to join him for the coming fight but, although some obeyed, the numbers were never large. After Irvine one could appreciate their hesitation at placing themselves under the command of someone they could quite easily see as a near fanatic, a frightening figure about to commit them to an all-out battle against the mighty English forces. If this was not enough, despite his changed relationship with his sponsors, he continued to profess personal loyalty to John Baliol. Although Baliol was still the titular king of the Scots he was in exile and had already shown an inability to stand up against his own nobles, let alone the English. Even Scottish nobles supporting the Baliol cause could hardly see any way back for John Baliol, living in restricted conditions in England and with his son held under lock and key in the Tower of London. In such circumstances one could forgive other Comyns for considering their own claims to the throne.

Apart from an understandable reluctance to accept the command of a young leader, other disturbing questions must have come into the mind of the highborn. For instance, did

Wallace support Baliol for reasons of naïve patriotism or because he had personal advantages in mind? In the unlikely event of a military victory following a hazardous battle, where their lives would be at great risk, could Wallace not set himself up as Baliol's direct representative?

As for that other main faction, the supporters of Robert Bruce, Bishop Wishart had already tasted Wallace's anger for his lack of commitment at Irvine, while it was asking a lot for the calculating James the Steward, Wallace's feudal overlord, to put himself unreservedly under Wallace's banner. In any case, was not Robert Bruce, the easy-going son of the Competitor, content to serve under Edward? Although, to general surprise, his twenty-two-year-old son (the future king) did join the revolt leading to Irvine, the knights of Annandale refused to follow him. It was only partly due to their absence that he failed to distinguish himself militarily, but if the knights of Annandale were unwilling to support the young Bruce before Irvine, how much more reluctant would they and other nobles be to join Wallace so soon after that disaster?

In the circumstances cautious individuals, while pleased to foment the revolt, continued to keep their options open and a proportion might still have preferred the prospect of life under the protection of a strong English king, rather than hazarding all on what they could justifiably see as a madcap enterprise doomed to almost certain failure.

Wallace would probably have been amazed if a large number of nobles had joined him. For Wallace, though, there was no luxury of holding back. The die was cast and the battlefield would seal the test of his leadership. Wallace moved north-wards to Dundee with some of his forces, probably the units of professional soldiers who had come over to him with their lord superiors. These were likely to have been mounted. Meanwhile, the bulk of his foot soldiers stayed in the forest of Selkirk, where they underwent extra training. It was Wallace's move north that provoked the English under the command of John

Warenne to respond, leaving their own safe haven of Berwick, and venture northwards in pursuit. After linking up with strong units under Hugh Cressingham, Edward's Scottish treasurer, the combined force set off to find and destroy the obstinate rebel. John of Fordun tells us that Wallace, having learned of their advance, broke off his siege of Dundee Castle and prepared to move towards Stirling, for he fully realised the significance of its river crossing.

A short time previously Wallace and Moray had met and made the sensible decision to work together, for undoubtedly the best way to counter a numerically larger and better-armed English army was to join forces. Accordingly both commanders, with their respective contingents, moved towards Stirling where at some point close by they must have been joined by Wallace's formations from the forest of Selkirk. Both guerrilla leaders were about to have the opportunity of demonstrating their military skills in a large-scale battle, particularly William Wallace in his role as overall commander.

CHAPTER FOUR

≈

STIRLING BRIDGE

> Now's the day and now's the hour
> See the front of battle lour
> See approach proud Edward's power –
> chains and slaverie.
>
> Robert Burns

T HE TWO ARMIES ABOUT to meet each other were markedly different. Despite the widely diverging estimates of the contemporary chroniclers it is likely that the combined forces of Moray and Wallace totalled at most 10,000[1] men with Moray's contingent likely to have been marginally the larger. For the most part they were foot soldiers. Although Moray and Wallace had already used horses successfully this was for greater speed of movement rather than as offensive weapons of war. At Stirling Bridge the Scottish cavalry was not only vastly inferior in numbers to its English opponents, but it was apparently kept under the separate control of nobles such as James the Steward and Malcolm, earl of Lennox, who, whilst pledging their support to the two young leaders, still wanted to keep their options open. As for the Scottish foot, they had been together for less than a month and the two main contingents coming from markedly different military backgrounds owed prime loyalty to their own commanders. Generally they were lightly armed and lacked formal military experience, their irregular operations over the last few months being far removed from pitched battles. The Scots had no recent military tradition to fall back on apart from the disastrous action at Dunbar twelve months before, when they put up little more than token resistance before being swept off the field. Due to the predominantly peaceful reigns of the kings the last instance of a fully contested action (and even this was more a skirmish than a true battle) had occurred against the Norsemen at Largs in 1263. There would be few active soldiers who still remembered it and far fewer who carried scars from it to Stirling Bridge.

On the credit side the Scots' infantry had two confident leaders of rare energy and spirit whom they trusted and under whom they had gained a string of successes, however minor some of them might be. Equally important the two men evidently showed a mutual respect for each other and unanimity of purpose, Moray selflessly allowing the senior leadership to be taken by Wallace. Above all they had the opportunity of choosing the battleground and of persuading the English to meet them on their terms.

Against the 10,000 Scots it has been estimated there were upwards of 50,000 English. With the serious logistic problems of supporting an army in Scotland and the undoubted confidence of the English after their facile victory at Dunbar this seems far too high a total, but they certainly had far superior numbers headed by a heavy striking force of some 2,000 armoured cavalry, against whom the Scottish cavalry was no match at all. Because the Scots had been discounted as a serious military threat the English raised soldiers only from counties north of the Trent, but their ranks included some veterans from earlier engagements in France and Palestine and also a company of the fierce and redoubtable Welsh bowmen.[2] The English forces had clear advantages but, with their formidable king elsewhere, there were weaknesses, too, notably in their high command.

John Warenne, earl of Surrey, the English commander-in-chief, was older than the two Scottish leaders combined and, while he had the advantage of a thorough training in the arts of war, this had been fully thirty years before. His leadership skills had hardly been tested at Dunbar although its outcome must have done wonders for his confidence. By no means fit, he was not overenthusiastic about field command in Scotland because he feared the country's cold damp airs were a menace to his health. Nor was Surrey on the best of terms with his arrogant vanguard commander, Hugh Cressingham, Edward's Scottish treasurer, whom he came to regard as someone unbecomingly eager to join battle at the earliest opportunity. Cressingham's problems by no means stopped with his senior commander; he was highly unpopular with the troops and despised by many of the nobles both as a bastard and a vain, self-opinionated man who had misappropriated for his own use some of the dues designated towards the rebuilding of Berwick.

Because of his reluctance to fight, Warenne took a number of initiatives prior to the battle in the hope of gaining a bloodless victory – actions hardly designed to increase confidence in his leadership or for that matter in his troops' enthusiasm for fighting. At Stirling the river Forth took a meandering course but it was still both wide and deep. While Warenne and his army, which had approached Stirling from the south, came up to the river barrier and gazed at the Scottish detachments on the far side, two of the Scots senior cavalry commanders, James the Steward and Malcolm, earl of Lennox, together with other Scottish barons, approached and offered to negotiate on Surrey's behalf with Wallace. The true motives of these men will probably never be clear. Perhaps with the memory of Dunbar fresh in their minds they felt Wallace had no chance and were registering their own loyalty to the English. Perhaps they were trying to prevent what they feared would be the inevitable destruction of the Scottish army. On the other hand they might have been trying to gain time for Wallace to confirm his tactical arrangements and strengthen his defensive position still further. They could even have been taking the chance of reporting back on the dispositions of the English forces.

Surrey agreed to their request but on the following day the self-appointed ambassadors returned and confessed they had failed to dissuade the two young men from fighting. What we know of Wallace and Moray makes it difficult to believe that the Steward and Lennox ever thought they could succeed in such an aim. However, the Steward and Lennox offered to join the English army on the next day (11 September 1297) along with forty knights, presumably after persuading them to change their allegiance. As they were leaving the English camp they met a group of English soldiers out foraging. A fracas occurred, during which Lennox drew his sword and badly wounded one of them. Angry English voices called for vengeance but Surrey, determined not to over-react, allowed the two Scots to depart peaceably, although he did promise that appropriate action would be taken against them if on the following morning they did not bring the promised reinforcements.

Surrey might well have concluded that while forty knights would not make much difference to his superiority in cavalry, their desertion would represent a disproportionately serious blow to the Scots. With or without them his plan was identical and that evening, in a pre-battle briefing, he outlined his field tactics to his officers. They were hardly complicated. After the English army crossed the Forth by the bridge which carried the main road north, they would form up on the flat low-lying ground and make a frontal attack on the Scottish forces occupying the higher ground. If unimaginative, the plan demonstrated confidence in his overwhelming superiority. On the day of the battle, however, the English leaders added amazing ineptitude to their lack of imagination. Early that morning some 5,000 infantry, together with a company of Welsh archers, successfully crossed the long narrow bridge, but Surrey himself was late in rising and the vanguard, lacking any orders to advance – or reaction from the Scots holding the daunting slopes west of Abbey Craig – returned. Surrey was apparently out of sorts physically but when he eventually made his leisurely appearance the army was paraded and, following normal practice, in the sight of everyone he created a number of new knights – many of whom were to fall that day.

The crossing had barely resumed before it was again reversed as the Steward and Lennox were seen returning from the Scottish position. There would be little point in forming up for the attack if they brought an offer of surrender. In reality there had, of course, never been any question of surrender – and the two came to admit their failure to detach other horsemen from the Scots army. Even now Surrey was reluctant to start fighting. Two Dominican friars were appointed to offer his official terms of surrender to Wallace and Moray. It was Wallace who replied, sure proof he was acknowledged as the senior commander. His words left the English no opportunity for confusion and no hope of compromise: 'Tell your people that we have not come here to gain peace, but are prepared for battle to avenge and deliver our country. Let them come up when they like, and they will find us ready to meet them to their beards.'[3] The friars had also been charged to spy out the land, although they were markedly incompetent here for, along with Wallace's message, they reported he had 180 mounted soldiers and up to 40,000 foot – a wild overestimate in the case of the infantry.

Perhaps it was this extravagant report together with the hesitation of their own commander, in stark contrast to the staunch message of the Scots under their fierce young leader, or perhaps it was the sight of the many pools of water in the meadows across the river which had an effect upon the English. Whatever the cause some now began to anticipate the serious problems in attempting to form up on the swampy, broken ground bounding both sides of the main road. They knew, too, that such manoeuvres would have to be performed under the gaze of the Scottish forces occupying formidably steep slopes abutting the even more dramatic feature of Abbey Craig. Standing today on the still swampy ground enclosed on three sides by the river, with the lowering crags of Abbey Craig directly in front, one is struck about the immense advantages for defence. Despite their high confidence the invaders were likely to have had similar thoughts (see map on page 54).

Whether motivated by the geography and dramatic atmosphere of the site, the tactical problems posed by it or inflated

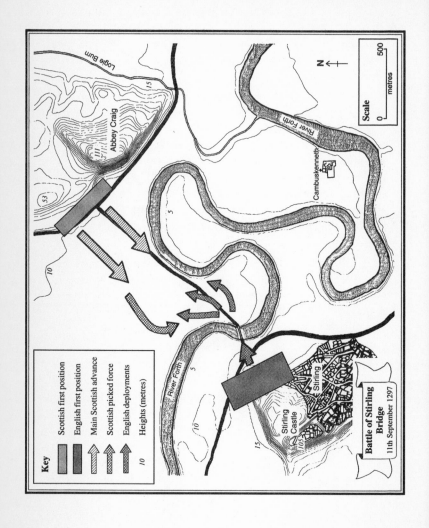

Key

Scottish first position
English first position
Main Scottish advance
Scottish picked force
English deployments
Heights (metres)

10

Abbey Craig

Logie Burn

River Forth

Cambuskenneth

River Forth

Stirling

Stirling

Stirling Castle

Battle of Stirling Bridge
11th September 1297

Scale

N

0   500
metres

estimates of the Scottish host, certain of the English staff officers began to doubt their sure prospects of success. One Scottish soldier, Sir Richard Lundie, who at Irvine had left the Scots in disgust because of their dissensions there, sounded a strong warning note against any renewed attempt to cross the narrow bridge: 'My Lords, if we cross that bridge now, we are all dead men. For we can only go over two abreast, and the enemy are already formed up: they can charge down on us whenever they wish.'[4] He proposed taking a formidable detachment of five hundred cavalry along with some infantry to a nearby ford, where sixty men could cross at a time. This force could then divert the Scots' attention from the main crossing by attacking them from behind.

Perhaps after his earlier treachery the English were understandably reluctant to accept Lundie's excellent advice but at this point Cressingham made his fatal intervention. Exasperated by the earlier delays and prolonged discussion about an attack against men he saw as no more than a group of brigands, irregulars who could hardly be expected to stand against the incomparable English cavalry supported by superior numbers of trained troops, he shouted to Surrey in sarcastic tones: 'There is no use, my lord Earl, in drawing out this business any longer, and wasting our King's revenues for nothing. Let us advance and carry out our duty as we are bound to do.'[5] What effect the argument about saving money might have had on Surrey can only be imagined but, irritated and weary of further discussion, he thereupon ordered Cressingham and his vanguard to start crossing the bridge and proceed with the frontal attack – all in full view of their enemy.

The proud English knights, on horses adorned with brightly embroidered saddle-cloths and accompanied by squires carrying their crested banners, clattered over the bridge two abreast until they emerged on the other side. Those who accomplished it successfully found themselves enclosed in a loop of the deep tidal river, while to their front and part straddling the main road the Scots gazed down on them. The English were occupying a position which gave them little opportunity to use their great superiority for, apart from the causeway which carried the main road, it was impossible to gallop horses on the soft hummocky ground to its flanks. Equally serious the area within the loop of the river was hardly large enough for them to use their infantry weapons effectively – and far too small to force the Scots, if they proposed to match them, to extend their own detachments unduly.

The river crossing was a protracted affair, it would have taken at least two hours and during all that time the Scots stood in silent anticipation. It says much for Wallace's powers of discipline and control (undoubtedly abetted here by Moray) that he could watch the English power steadily growing, consisting as it did not only of their fearsome mailed knights but spearmen and the famed Welsh archers, too. Finally, as Hemingburgh expressed it, 'when as many of the enemy had come over as they believed they could overcome', Wallace gave the signal to attack. Blind Harry described it as coming from a single blast on his horn:

> In all the host suld no man blaw but he.

When Wallace sounded the attack he was likely to have been standing on Abbey Craig, where both sets of forces were spread out below him, before spurring his horse down its steep banks to join his own troops. At the signal the whole Scots force set off, shouting hoarsely. The committed among them uttered their clan battle cries or called on 'Blessed St Margaret', while others used a variety of oaths to give themselves greater courage and strike fear into their opponents. Down the slopes they came, keeping their formations. Then they turned down the axis of the road causeway and being lightly armed leapt across the humps in the water meadows to close with the enemy. On this day they were irresistible. This time it was far from Dunbar's blind rush by men eager to crush the English; the tactics were soundly planned. While the main body crashed into opponents not yet fully drawn up for battle, a picked force of spearmen on the right wing of the army went straight for the bridge itself. Their duty was to prevent further reinforcements and to block any English withdrawal. They succeeded in reaching it as the English reeled back from the crashing force of the main Scottish charge. Already some of the invaders, too closely packed to fight properly, were giving way to panic. Accounts vary about the state of the bridge. Blind Harry, for instance, has Wallace weakening it to bring about a collapse under the great weight of the English forces. This seems unlikely, for it would scarcely have given Wallace the vital control over the battle which he sought. Others have the Scots detachment which seized the far end hacking at it until it collapsed. Although accounts persist that the bridge was partly demolished, what can be taken for certain is that the bulk of the English force did not recross successfully. The chroniclers refer to only one English cavalry commander, Sir Marmaduke Twenge, keeping his head amid the murderous mêlée. After first driving back some Scottish horse who approached him from the flank, he succeeded in reversing his body of knights. With Twenge at their head, followed directly by his squire carrying a mortally wounded man, they galloped back along the road axis towards the Scots contingent holding the bridge. Cutting and barging their way through it, they regained the bridge and were able to pass over to rejoin the main English army. It needs little imagination to visualise Twenge's heavy horses – after first beating back the Scots – crashing their way along the narrow, sloping bridge and scattering English foot soldiers in their path. Many would doubtless have been pushed into the water. With the exception of this cavalry squadron the Scottish block held, acting as an anvil to the bludgeoning attackers. Caught between the two, more than 5,000 English infantrymen, including archers, and more than 100 horsemen, died. Finding themselves driven into the shallows many attempted to swim the river but only a handful succeeded.

On the Scottish side the battle of Stirling Bridge was a

notable success for the two young leaders and for Wallace, in particular. He had shown the mark of other pre-eminent commanders in being not merely content to inspire his own troops but eager to judge and measure the qualities of his opponents. By replying to Surrey's two religious ambassadors as he did, he made sure the noble lord could hardly refuse the challenge and made it more likely that hot-heads among his English army would have their way over the unimaginative frontal attack.

Some commentators have questioned Wallace's powers of imagination, to them his words were the natural ones of a patriotic leader. This is less than generous for he had already shown himself a cunning fighter, even if his actions had been on a much smaller scale. No one can deny his choice of ground at Stirling was brilliant and the control exercised over his still inexperienced forces, a portion of whom had served under him only briefly, was equally or more creditable. So, too, was his timing – he kept his nerve against what in the thirteenth century would have been forces equivalent to those of a modern superpower – and waited until the English had irrevocably committed themselves. He then struck before they could bring over more troops than he could cope with. Wallace saw clearly that his attack had first to close the jaws of the trap by securing the far end of the bridge before compressing the better equipped and more professional enemy forces on unfavourable and restricted ground.

As for the English commanders, the battle could hardly have been worse. The arrogant Cressingham paid with his life, while Surrey, like the greater part of his army on the other side of the bridge, experienced a soldier's worst nightmare. He had to watch his comrades being hacked and killed not much more than one hundred yards away without being able to do a thing about it. It must have been a horrifying and sickening sight. Surrey and others among the English had experienced the excitement of a successful cavalry charge on other fields. But when walled in by opponents lunging and scything at them, this most fearsome of war weapons became notably ineffective. Their horses' bellies were all too vulnerable for Scots' dirks and plunging, screaming stallions with their entrails hanging out were no safe platforms. As their riders were brought crashing to the ground, whether pinned under their horses or not, they made relatively easy prey for men unencumbered by heavy mail. As for the archers, to make their deadly weapons count they needed space between themselves and their opponents. At Stirling the headlong charge of the Scots into the English ranks denied them this. With their prime weapons negated they, too, were at a marked disadvantage against men used to sword and lance-play.

Surrey and his fellow commanders had to watch their magnificent army, which so recently had swept the Scots off the field, itself being ground to pieces in the brutal hand-to-hand fighting before Stirling Bridge. To their despair they had to acknowledge that, while Wallace's men might be relatively untrained in contemporary warfare, they fought with a raw energy and an anger which their own more specialist troops could not match. It could hardly have escaped them that nothing but a victory would do for the Scots. If English knights were unhorsed and captured they could expect to be ransomed. For most of the others who survived the battle of Stirling Bridge there would be the expectation of a successful expedition the next year under the king. For the Scottish infantry, a proportion of them outlaws, led by a man also declared as an outlaw, there could be no second chance. Defeat could mean only death, if not on the battlefield itself, then hunted down later in a country which the English meant to subjugate entirely.

For all English observers that day, whether they had made any attempt to understand the behaviour of the opposition, or not, the relish the Scots showed for fighting and their implacability must have been awesome. Being so close to the action, along with the sights, Surrey and the others would have heard telling sounds of battle: the grunts of exertion as men swung swords, thrust spears or grappled together, the thud of stout staves upon bone and muscle, the cries of men as their flesh was pared to the bone or faces changed into the blood red meat of a butcher's block. These would surely be accompanied by others: the clashing of swords, the screams of terrified horses, the thrashing of men trying to keep their footing in the riverside pools, the frenzied sound of sergeants trying to restore order and the splash of bodies falling from the bridge into the river below.

With the sights and sounds of the English force diminishing would come the realisation that growing numbers of the enemy were lining the river bank before them. Even with their vanguard gone the English had ample strength to meet the Scots and hold them off. But the nightmare scene inevitably took its toll. They had lost the initiative and realised these devils did not fight like ordinary men or like their counterparts so recently humiliated at Dunbar. Even now they might be using the fords to cut them off. With such fears in mind some English detachments began to filter southwards. Most disgraceful of all Surrey who, in the first place, had been so reluctant to start fighting had plainly lost all appetite for it. Along with his bodyguard he galloped south as fast as he could apparently closely pursued in the process. His headlong flight only ceased at Berwick, from where he had recently set out with such justifiable confidence but fatal underestimation of Scottish resolve under Wallace. According to the chroniclers, at Berwick his proud warhorse dropped dead from the use he made of it. Before he fled, Surrey put Stirling Castle into the joint hands of Sir Marmaduke Twenge and Sir William Fitzwarine. One can only speculate on his decision here. Perhaps Sir Marmaduke was just close by. Perhaps Surrey hoped that by using Twenge's cool-headedness and military talents he would be able to preserve it for longer than could reasonably be expected. There is even the possibility that he would have preferred Twenge, along with the others, to have met a soldier's death on the far side of the bridge. Whatever

Surrey's motive the task of holding Stirling Castle, when other English forces had retreated to the border, was a decidedly short straw. Sure enough Twenge's provisions soon ran out and he had to surrender. Luckily for him Wallace the implacable, displaying a chivalrous quality which some of his enemies denied he ever possessed, recognised Twenge as a courageous soldier and spared both his life and that of Fitzwarine.

On the Scottish side the high-born men who might have been thought of as the obvious leaders hardly distinguished themselves in the battle. Although at the beginning of the engagement the Steward and the earl of Lennox rejoined their followers, they occupied a different station from the army's main body and were described as 'lurking in the woods near the hills'.[6] One can only guess what their actions might have been if the day had gone against Wallace, but when they saw Surrey fleeing they joined in the pursuit, killing many and taking large quantities of booty.

As with other overwhelming victories the Scottish casualties were comparatively light with the one terrible exception of Andrew Moray. Wallace's co-leader received a wound from which he was to die two months later, although up to the very time of Moray's death Wallace included his name on proclamations of state.

The battle of Stirling Bridge has additional interest for two other reasons. It opened a new chapter in the conduct of war, breaking one of the basic precepts of the Middle Ages that the command of an army should be the privilege of those with noble blood. At Stirling Bridge, Wallace, the younger son of a modest knight – admittedly supported by a scion from one of Scotland's leading families – succeeded in defeating an English army led by a noble earl despite its much greater numbers and more experienced troops.

It also broke the current rules of behaviour to the dead. After he had been killed the Scots stripped the skin off Cressingham's body. This followed no chivalric code. That Wallace allowed it raises a number of questions. Had the deaths of his father, brother and wife made him an angry, stern man, as Blind

Harry suggested, or was he just an unyielding patriot, dedicated to fighting without pause or quarter anyone he considered threatened the existence of his country? One is led to doubt whether such behaviour against Cressingham would have been tolerated had Moray not been seriously injured. And while it is just conceivable that Wallace's royal adversary, Edward I, might in extreme circumstances have had infidels flayed alive – it was scarcely much worse than his practice of hanging, drawing and quartering traitors – he would already have made the 'punishment' part of his legal code. Wallace's conduct against a dead enemy was quite different. Such savagery made more sense against tyrants and perhaps Wallace, with some justification, regarded the English invaders as such. In these circumstances he might have reasoned that by sending strips of Cressingham's skin across Scotland his victory at Stirling Bridge would be announced in a most dramatic fashion, and as an unforgettable reminder of his determination to others less convinced or committed than himself. We have no evidence that this was so. The chances are that the iron control he could impose on his savage men during the battle was relaxed in the aftermath of success.

It comes as no surprise that the chroniclers made much of Cressingham's flaying. The bitterly hostile accounts from Lanercost priory even went so far as to accuse Wallace of causing 'a broad strip to be taken from the head to the heel, to make therewith a baldrick for his sword'.[7] This is not proven and, in any case, with his huge sword, human skin would hardly have been strong enough. Another chronicler, Walter of Guisborough, stated that they 'divided his skin among themselves in moderate sized pieces, certainly not as relics, but for hatred of him'.[8] This seems far more credible. Whatever the truth it was savage conduct which brought an understandably fierce reaction from south of the border.

While the battle of Stirling Bridge had important military and political consequences it did not, of itself, end the war. Nor for that matter would the next battle. By this time hatred between the Scots and English went far too deep and a developing sense of Scottish nationalism had become irreversible. Militarily Stirling enabled all the towns – though not the castles – still in English hands to be recaptured and brought new respect for Scottish fighting potential under Wallace. In the words of the nineteenth century Scottish historian, Patrick Fraser Tytler: 'Thus by the efforts of a single man, not only unassisted but actually thwarted and opposed by the nobility of the country was the iron power of Edward completely broken and Scotland once more able to lift her head among free nations.'[9]

While at the moment of victory, and shortly after the battle, this might be true, no one could imagine that England, under such a strong king and with a population five times greater than Scotland's, would long accept such a humiliation. The very manner of the Scottish victory warranted a quick reaction. When the battle took place a major threat of civil war existed in England, with the earls of Hereford and Norfolk, together with their followers, openly in arms against the king. The seat of the troubles lay with the question of the royal prerogative to impose heavy and seemingly arbitrary taxation together with his imperious demands for feudal service overseas. But Surrey's humiliation and the treatment of Cressingham's body were insults that united the country against the Scots.

In their vituperation against Wallace the chroniclers and popular songs of the period reflected the prevailing mood. Yet England's military response was less quick than some might have wished. Although large numbers of men began to be raised, Wallace's reputation prevented the English undertaking any new campaign until their king returned from the Continent to take personal command. Wallace's victory gave him precious but limited time to develop a greater sense of national awareness amongst all classes, especially the common people, and to prepare a military force equal to the coming challenge. In the meantime, during the late autumn and early winter of 1297, he took his army on a punitive raid into the English border counties. Through this he hoped to keep the nucleus of his army together during the inclement months while at the same time satisfying his own wish to visit the horrors of warfare on England. Those taking part could also bring back considerable loot to help some of the Scottish regions survive the winter, particularly those devastated by war. Understandably, the English chroniclers and rhymers again took the opportunity to arouse popular emotion against Wallace with the Lanercost Chronicle characteristically in the forefront here:

> Welsh William being made a noble
> Straight way the Scots became ignoble
> Treason and slaughter, arson and raid
> By suffering and misery must be repaid.[10]

It is therefore of interest to find that although Walter of Hemingburgh joined in relating the sufferings which Wallace's troops caused, he also gave some indication of Wallace's more noble side: showing him protecting monks at Hexham, celebrating mass with them and later ordering his soldiers to be punished for snatching relics from that place. This accorded with reports from the supportive Scottish sources – not only his champion Blind Harry – that Wallace invariably showed mercy to women and children. Unsurprisingly, John of Fordun strongly emphasised the legitimacy of Wallace's actions, together with references to his religious faith and respect for the defenceless:

'On account of which God was with him through whom he was successful in all his undertakings; in as much as he revered the church, honoured the ecclesiastics, supported the poor and the widows, cherished the fatherless and the orphans, relieved the oppressed, detected thieves and robbers and without reward inflicted upon them strict justice.'[11]

Within Scotland by far the most important event to unify Scottish resolve following Stirling was Wallace's knighting (carried out by a senior baron, possibly even Bruce) and the revival of the post of Guardian with Wallace elected to it. As Guardian of the Kingdom, although technically subject to John Baliol, his powers were equivalent to those taken later by Cromwell as Protector of the Commonwealth. Officially Wallace started by being co-Guardian with Andrew Moray but, although directives issued until the end of November 1297 were given in both their names, Moray died by the end of the month.

In March 1298 Wallace was referred to as 'Guardian by consent of the community of the Kingdom'. The importance of these words was the acceptance by the Scottish nobles, the great feudal magnates among them, of directives from the junior knight William Wallace about resisting the English.[12] What proportion consented will never be known but it must have been a representative one including the senior prelates of the day. Equally certain, a proportion would have opposed the elevation of such a young and inexperienced man. And yet, in spite of his junior capacity, they could not deny he had proved his country's military champion. Most of the dissenters probably thought it wise to keep silent over their disapproval, knowing the opportunity to raise their voices would come with a military setback. Meanwhile, lack of positive support would make it more likely.

As for Wallace himself his enthusiasm went without asking and there would have been strong approval for his appointment from within the burghs and among the rural freeholders. The obsequious abbot, Walter Bower, made no bones about Wallace's high leadership qualities and the general support they served to attract: 'he won over to himself the grace and favour of the hearts of all loyal Scots . . . for he was most liberal in his gifts, very fair in his judgements, most compassionate in comforting the sad, a skilful counsellor, very patient when suffering, a distinguished speaker, who above all hunted down falsehood and deceit and detested treachery, for this reason the Lord was with him . . .'[13]

Whatever breadth of support Wallace enjoyed he dared not react vindictively to the continuing and powerful opposition of some who either chose to ignore the full dangers posed by the English, or refused to accept the new current of patriotic feeling within Scotland. To the surprise of many he remained even-handed, if habitually stern. Although the office of Guardian placed immense responsibilites on someone quite untried in such areas, his precocious maturity and leadership skills soon became evident. Above all, men could see that he did not lack courage or self-confidence. As a committed patriot facing a mortal threat to his country Wallace saw no need for false modesty. His own strong leadership was necessary because members from the senior nobility had felt unable to assume their responsibilities. This was entirely understandable when their families and estates had fallen into the hands of the English king, and hardly less so when they refused to co-operate with their political opponents, as was the case with the Bruce and the Balliol factions.

Wallace knew he had only a short interval before an avenging English king would attack again and this time Wallace himself would be an especial target. Important decisions had to be made and quickly. Greater unanimity of purpose within the kingdom needed to be encouraged and a national military force raised. This time Wallace had to prepare to meet – and beat – the whole English army, not just its vanguard and one led by an experienced and skilled leader who would demand feudal allegiance from many Scottish nobles.

In the meantime there were wider considerations: other countries had to be assured that Scotland was free again and wished to renew both its political and economic links with northern Europe. Despite the limited evidence available it is possible to gain some impression of the heroic efforts which Wallace made to prepare his country during the ten months allowed him between the battle of Stirling Bridge and the battle of Falkirk during July of the following year. Immediately after taking up his great office he sought a renewal of international trade. On 11 October 1297 European countries such as Norway, Flanders, France and the Hanseatic League were reminded that a free Scotland was a worthwhile trading partner. A letter of that date to Lübeck, the chief city of the Hanseatic League, was headed 'Andrew de Moray and William Wallace, leaders of the army of the Kingdom of Scotland and the community of the same Kingdom . . . request you that you will be pleased to make it known among your merchants that they can have safe access to all the ports of the Kingdom of Scotland with their merchandize; for the Kingdom of Scotland, God be thanked, has been recovered by war from the power of the English.'[14] Wallace declared that Scotland was back in business. In all probability additional letters written in the same fashion were sent to the country's other regular trading partners.

Within Scotland Wallace attempted to place his own clients, strong patriots, into important positions of power and during the autumn, though he was occupied with military matters in England he somehow made time for such appointments. Wallace fully realised the importance of the Church in fostering national resistance and his outstanding decision concerned a senior ecclesiastical official. On Wallace's instructions the appointment of William Comyn, brother of the earl of Buchan, into the country's pre-eminent bishopric at St Andrews, was overturned in favour of his own candidate, William Lamberton. It was done in the nick of time for, while Comyn had already been elected, he was yet to be consecrated.

There are good reasons to believe Wallace also rewarded laymen who had distinguished themselves against the English oppressors, although there is evidence here of a single charter only. This was given by Wallace to one Alexander Scrymgeour, a brave soldier who, on 29 March 1298, was confirmed as hereditary royal standard bearer and constable of Dundee Castle, with rights to certain lands in the neighbourhood of Dundee.

John of Fordun's reference to Wallace bringing 'all the magnates in Scotland under his sway' must have involved a series of national directives and in certain cases even more forceful means. Wallace showed himself not only supremely confident here but he totally disregarded their powers of opposition. As John of Fordun expressed it: 'Such of the magnates, morever, as did not thankfully obey his commands he took and browbeat and handed over to custody, until they should utterly submit to his good pleasure.'[15] It was surely a measure of Wallace's stamp of authority that when Edward summoned the Scottish nobles to attend an English parliament at York, the first time in January 1298 and then in May of the same year, not one obeyed. Yet as Walter of Guisborough had observed, Wallace 'was deemed base-born by the Lords and Nobles'[16] and such strong treatment would lead to sulky acquiescence rather than support freely given. In the short time available to him he had little alternative.

Politically, Wallace might have felt that he had done everything possible under the circumstances: he had alerted Europe to Scotland's re-emergence and its wish to resume trading relations and, largely through his appointment of Bishop Lamberton who was scheduled to go to Rome for his consecration, he hoped he might be able to enlist powerful support from both the Pope and the French king.

All such initiatives, however, were less important than being able to create a land army fit to face and beat the English. In the thirteenth century, performance on the battlefield was by far the most important gauge of a country's independence. Through his victory at Stirling Bridge Wallace had been able to resume normal political relations with the rest of Europe and had succeeded in clearing English troops from the country. If he could defeat the English army under its formidable king he would be able to confirm Scotland's independence by a treaty which the Pope and the chief European powers would surely demand. If he was defeated, Scotland would once again be occupied, its identity as a separate state brought into serious question and the allegiance of its chief men captured by the English king on grounds both of conquest and superior feudal lordship.

Thus far Wallace had demonstrated his great military ability with footsoldiers who, for the most part, owed strong allegiance to himself or Andrew Moray. He must have wondered whether he could do equally well with an army containing more contingents of men, including cavalry, whose first loyalty was to their own lords superior. Would they be amenable, for instance, to his own demanding levels of discipline? If they failed to meet his standards and refused to accept further training could he dismiss them? In practice this situation did not arise for only a disappointingly small number of nobles became his active supporters and brought their soldiery to join him. The names were few enough: the most notable being MacDuff, the great-uncle of the earl of Fife; John Stewart, younger brother of the Steward; Sir John Graham of Dundaff; Robert Boyd; Henry of Haliburton; Sir Nichol de Rutherford; and John Comyn the Red (along with a small body of cavalry). However, Evan Barron maintains that some others, namely the earls of Atholl, Menteith, Buchan, Lennox and Carrick also contributed contingents to the army.[17]

Even so, these were still quite unable to fill his battle lines. As at Stirling, Wallace had to rely mainly on others who were relatively untrained, such as dispossessed landowners and peasants, small farmers, minor lairds and townsmen not under the control of a feudal superior. Walter Bower goes further and suggests that Wallace attempted to increase and extend his pool of men by a general summons for the Scottish host which cut across the system of feudal vassalage. By this he divided the country into military districts and compiled muster rolls containing the names of all males aged between sixteen and sixty.[18] Whether such men were vassals or not their superiors were obliged to release them for the army. Wallace enforced this regulation by a decree of state that not only in every barony but in every town 'a gallows should be erected on which all without a reasonable cause absenting themselves from the army under foreign pretexts should be hanged'. To prove his determination, Wallace went north to deal with 'certain recalcitrants' who refused to carry out his orders and hanged a number who defied him.[19]

With a limited number of cavalry, about whose loyalty he was by no means sure, Wallace was compelled once more to put his trust in infantry soldiers, many of whom were untrained. Before they could meet the English it was vital they acquired battlefield drills and developed a strong sense of mutual cohesion. Such an army would have to adopt formations which could frustrate enemy cavalry but still carry out his tactical requirements, including offensive action. The soundness of whatever arrangements he could make here would shortly be tested in battle, and this time he would no longer have the valuable support of his great lieutenant, Andrew Moray. As Blind Harry put it, 'for Wallace the time of trial was close'.

CHAPTER FIVE

≈

FALKIRK

I am tied to the stake and I must stand the course.

Shakespeare, *King Lear*

THERE HAS BEEN AN understandable tendency for commentators to give unstinting praise to Wallace for his conduct at Stirling Bridge and too little credit for his arrangements at Falkirk. Evan Barron, ever anxious to enhance the reputation of his hero, Moray, even goes so far as to suggest that Falkirk should never have been fought because the tactics there were the antithesis of those which succeeded at Stirling Bridge. This argument seems hardly convincing for, whilst not denigrating the joint triumph of the two leaders at Stirling Bridge, tactics have to be adapted to different circumstances and success against Surrey would always be easier than against Edward I leading English forces seeking revenge.

Wallace's adversaries at Stirling were not only at odds with each other but they blithely underestimated the ability of the two young Scottish leaders. At Falkirk Wallace faced a proud English king who, while hardly one of the world's greatest commanders, was immensely experienced, personally courageous and a man who would certainly not allow indiscipline from his detachment commanders. By now Edward would also have no illusions about Wallace's ability and would therefore be the more determined to bring him to battle. At Stirling, while the location had been most carefully chosen by the defenders, the English showed crass incompetence and by not using other river crossings, thrust themselves into an obvious trap. At Falkirk it would be different with the English rushing the Scots into fighting on a position which, although favourable for defence, was hardly comparable with that at Stirling.

At Stirling the English high command had been divided by serious differences over starting the battle, whereas at Falkirk all were eager to get to grips with the Scots and have their revenge. Despite serious troubles with the Welsh soldiers immediately prior to it, they were eventually able to take an important part in Falkirk's crucial stages. On the Scottish side, in contrast to the important role played by the cavalry in Stirling's final stages, at Falkirk they deserted early on. Any skills Wallace might have had in deploying mounted forces were not fully tested because the nobles refused to place themselves under his control. Whereas Stirling Bridge was a brilliant encounter battle, Falkirk occurred at the end of a carefully planned campaign and cannot be considered independently of the actions preceding it.

At Falkirk, as in all battles, whatever the leadership skills the composition of the two armies went far to determine the outcome. Frustratingly our knowledge here is decidedly one-sided. We know that once again the English had superior numbers in infantry but especially in cavalry. Among their infantry were 10,000 Welsh longbowmen with an additional 2,000 men from Chester and Lancashire and 600 or so crossbowmen, half of whom were Gascon mercenaries. With regard to the cavalry, some 1,300 were professionals, paid men, including mounted mercenaries from Gascony, while a further 1,100 were nobles and their retinues, supporting their feudal master the king, a total of 2,400 in all.[1] According to the detailed study that John Morris has made of the muster rolls, the English infantry had a numerical superiority of some 30 per cent, while their preponderance in cavalry was much higher, probably in the order of six to one. They also had qualitative superiority in both arms, for many of their foot soldiers had seen service in previous campaigns and over 50 per cent of the cavalry were full-time. Apart from the superior range and hitting power of their archers, both longbowmen and crossbowmen, their infantry generally had a better array of personal weapons than the twelve-foot lances which, sometimes supplemented by short dirks and axes, were carried by the vast proportion of the Scots.

By contrast, relatively little is known about the men who made up the Scottish ranks. Fergusson puts the majority as coming from Ayrshire and Galloway, together with some from the devastated border area. He quotes Robert de Brunne's metrical chronicle – which itself scarcely makes things crystal clear – that apart from Ayrshire, others of Wallace's troops would have come from quite different locations – Scotland, Galloway, the North and the Isles, for instance. (The Scotland referred to here was the district north of the Forth and some of the men from the north would very probably have been those who came with Andrew Moray, transferring their allegiance after his death to Wallace, while the men of the Isles is probably a reference to Sir John Stewart's men of Bute.) Unfortunately, the Scottish chroniclers' accounts of the battle are vitiated by the amount of time they spent trying to blame specific leaders: on the one hand the Comyns who, with their retinues, quit the field and on the other Robert Bruce, whom they accused of actively working with the English.[2] For the Scots the numerical imbalance might have been far worse if the English had not faced such extreme difficulties over provisioning men in a country lacking both food and fodder.

Given the two commanders' vastly different levels of experience and the unequal nature of their armies, the Scots appeared to stand no chance of winning a set battle unless they could find a way of levelling the odds against them. The two best chances seemed to lie in taking up a position which was virtually impregnable and again persuading the English to attack it or, by skilful use of their country's geography, in avoiding a great set battle and bringing the English to a state approaching exhaustion and despair.

One can hardly doubt that in the circumstances Wallace, a

master of guerrilla warfare, would have been strongly tempted to avoid a set battle and, following the earlier example of the Roman general Fabius Cunctator, would try to entice the English into inhospitable country where he could interrupt their food supplies and cut off their stragglers until they lost the will to fight. Such methods could scarcely be popular with many of his followers, especially the hot-blooded Celts from the north, nor to the liking of the nobles who provided his cavalry units. However, these were the tactics he adopted during the best part of July as the English moved blindly northwards, their every move watched by his scouts and local spies. By them he succeeded in reducing the English army to near starvation. Along with their physical difficulties they also suffered serious problems of morale.

Why then did he fight where he did? It is Evan Barron's contention – and one which is difficult to challenge – that Wallace had no need to meet the English on a modest hill near Falkirk and that, if a set battle had always been Wallace's objective, he would surely have chosen a better position. Yet, once the English learned where he was and eagerly sought battle he seemed content to give it. Wallace might, of course, have been pressured into it by his fellow leaders, especially the senior nobles among his cavalry to whom avoiding tactics would have been both non-chivalrous and demeaning. On the other hand, the information coming to him from his scouts, that the English were at their last gasp and suffering serious dissensions among their foreign troops, might have persuaded him that the time for battle had arrived.

It should be borne in mind, too, that Wallace was fully justified in seeing the English king as the source of virtually all his country's sufferings since the succession crisis. If he continued to delay, the English might well be forced to break off the campaign for that year but, unless effective diplomatic pressures could be exerted from other seats of power in Europe, they would be back during the next year, and the next, and the next. By beating Edward himself in battle rather than his inferior lieutenant, Surrey, Wallace could free Scotland from English troops, bring wavering Scottish earls over to the cause of their home country, confirm his own position – and complete his life's work. It was a glittering prospect for any young man. Another reason for fighting where he did was likely to have been his belief that he had found another means of reducing the heavy odds, for he had already drilled his infantry in a formation reminiscent of the ancient Greek phalanx: the schiltron, a unit of 2,000 or so men, each armed with twelve-foot spears described by the chronicler Walter of Guisborough as standing 'shoulder to shoulder in deep ranks and facing towards the circumference of the circle, with their spears slanting outwards at an oblique angle'. The chronicler Hemingburgh gives more detail still. He tells us that Wallace created four circular formations, each consisting of a double rank facing outwards, the front one crouching or sitting on the ground with their spears slanting upwards and the second standing directly behind, inclining their weapons over the heads of the front rank. At the centre of the circle there was likely to be a reserve ready to fill any gaps that might appear in the spear wall. Like the earlier Greek phalanx the full advantage of such a formidable hedgehog-like formation was its ability to switch from defence to attack, but to do this its soldiers' standard of drill had to be high and the ground relatively smooth. During the previous winter as he weighed the arguments for adopting the schiltron formation Wallace must have been conscious of the recent English success at Maes Moydog against a dense formation of Welsh spearmen by using cavalry closely supported by crossbowmen. This must surely have influenced his decision to support his own spear walls with bowmen, although the only Scottish archers he could raise were the men from the Ettrick Forest with their short bows. Under Wallace's scheme for battle the bowmen would themselves be protected by the Scottish cavalry positioned to the flanks and rear of the schiltrons.

How, despite his military inexperience, he came to adopt

such a revolutionary formation has never been answered satisfactorily. It might have been suggested to him by an experienced old hand among his followers, or perhaps even by Andrew Moray, but it was Wallace himself who had the vision and determination to adopt the system. Whether he could use it to its full effect was far less certain. His heavy responsibilities as sole Guardian would have restricted his personal involvement in the preparatory training and in all likelihood he appointed drill supervisors for the purpose. However, no one can accuse Wallace of not making full use of the interval between Stirling Bridge and Falkirk. And it has to be acknowledged that the schiltron was not only a proven solution for infantry against superior cavalry but also an effective formation for relatively raw soldiers who could take heart from the closeness of their comrades and the encouragement and commands of their sergeants. Far less certain in this case was the ability of such men to change from a defensive to an attacking role and hanging over them was the immense superiority of the English and Welsh longbowmen.

At Falkirk the preliminaries were important. When King Edward and his English troops entered Scotland, the Scots gave way, carrying out scorched-earth tactics as they fell back. By the time the English reached the Forth at Kirkliston near Queensferry, they were sorely in need of provisions. These were due to come from Berwick but adverse weather conditions delayed the fleet and Scottish raiding parties had interrupted supplies moving along the coast road. As a result the army was close to starvation. The situation was near desperate, but Edward refused to be deterred and called on his men to destroy three castles which were the source of the attacks on their supply lines. One of these was at Dirleton and another was probably Hailes, occupying a rocky eminence above the Tyne. When a messenger from his fighting prelate, the bishop of Durham, asked the king for instructions he ordered the bishop not to hold back. 'Tell the bishop that in so far as he is a bishop he is a good man, but that his goodness is out of place for this task.' To one of them, a particularly savage knight named Sir John Fitz-Marmaduke, he was even more specific: 'You are a cruel man, and I have several times rebuked you for being too cruel, and for the pleasure you take in the death of your enemies. But now go and exert all your frightfulness and I shall not even blame you, but praise you. And mind you do not see my face again until these three castles are burnt.'[3]

The three castles quickly passed into English hands (in fact two of them were abandoned), but when the bishop of Durham rejoined the king he found the army still desperate for food. A limited number of supply carts had got through from Leith but they carried more wine than food, and when the wine was distributed to the famished Welsh detachment they became both drunk and offensive, physically abusing priests and others alike. Orders were given to drive them out of the main camp and in the process some were killed. Understandably they became angry and mutinous but Edward, when this was reported to him, snapped out, 'What do I care if my enemies join my enemies? Let them go where they like: with God's help I shall be revenged on both of them in one day.'[4] Despite such bravado the army's state was, if anything, worse than before and, in a desperate attempt to preserve its morale, Edward let it be known he was about to retire to Edinburgh where food was available. Not until the men had been fed would he decide about resuming his march.

Wallace was well aware of the enemy's difficulties and his reaction was that of a guerrilla leader rather than an orthodox commander of the time. He decided to hasten the English army's disintegration by attacking its rearguard. To achieve this he had to keep his men within reasonable marching distance.

On the other side Edward, operating in a hostile country, enjoyed far less accurate intelligence. He had not yet caught a glimpse of Wallace's troops during the campaign so far and, what with this and the grave difficulties over provisions, even he must have been feeling disheartened. However, at dawn on

21 July, a boy sent out as a spy by the earls of March and Angus was brought to him and gave him vital news. This was that the Scots, having learned he intended falling back on Edinburgh, meant to follow and attack the English camp the next night, or failing this to fall on their rearguard and plunder their vanguard whilst they were on the march. More serious still for the Scots the boy told Edward that 'the Scots army and all your enemies are no more than eighteen miles from here, near Falkirk'.[5] This was the chance Edward had been vigorously praying for and he cried out, 'God be praised who has brought me out of every strait! They shall have no need to follow me for I shall go to meet them, and on this very day.'[6]

His troops were ordered to take up their arms and be prepared to march. Mounting his charger the king himself gave the lead and by nine o'clock that morning the whole army was on the move. After a full day's march they camped just outside Linlithgow and, with a surprise attack from the Scots ever in their minds, lay on their arms. For the knights this meant keeping their horses close by them. As they were all stallions they could easily become excitable. Such was the case for during the night the king's charger, becoming alarmed, broke loose and trampled upon his master, apparently breaking two of his ribs. The news of the king's injury spread alarm through the army, and calm was restored only when Edward, despite the pain he must have been suffering, mounted his charger and, although it was still dark, ordered the advance to be resumed. One is forced to wonder how many other men of fifty-nine in the thirteenth century, after a life of great exertions, would have acted with such resolution and speed? Such was the calibre of the opponent who sought William Wallace on St Mary Magdalene's day compared with a vacillating Surrey the year before.

After a further march of some six to seven miles, as the first rays of dawn were lightening the sky the English caught sight of what they thought were forward Scottish detachments.

Edward called a halt and ordered mass to be celebrated; there was no point in blundering into a trap and in a religious age such a dedication was bound to raise morale. When the service was over it was light enough for the English to see the Scottish army on a hill to their front apparently being drawn up for battle. Whether, after resting under the cover of the nearby woods, the Scots had come out to occupy carefully pre-selected positions or through a last-minute choice they were reversing a decision to withdraw still further will, of course, never be known. What evidence there is points to the latter case. If the Scots had been set on fighting at that place it is surprising, at the least, that they had not already decided on the shape of their defensive formations.

The actual site of the battlefield remains uncertain. Some commentators have placed it north of Falkirk, Blind Harry put it on Slamannan Muir to the south-west of the town and James Fergusson puts it more directly south on the river Avon. Local historians now incline to a position much nearer Falkirk. The site favoured by John Walker (and after walking the area this is the site I favour) is on the hillside of Mumrills Brae, the site of a Roman fort on the Antonine Wall. This adjoins the traditional route from Linlithgow to Falkirk and is protected on three sides by the Westquarter Burn which is steepest on the west. To the north and west are woods at Westquarter and Lauriston which, in the thirteenth century, were very likely to have been connected with Callendar Wood and to have offered a likely escape route. While a possible site to the immediate north-west of Wallacestone cannot be utterly discarded, the area of Mumrills Brae offers the more satisfactory features and fits more closely with contemporary descriptions.

Although it might seem surprising that no hard evidence has been uncovered of this considerable battle, no bones would survive in the acidic soil, while weapons and other possessions would have been scavenged by the local population. Coming before the use of gunpowder there would have been neither bullets nor cannon balls. There are some – Geoffrey Bailey, experienced archaeologist and curator of Falkirk Museum among them – who believe the site, like that of the famed Scottish battle of Mons Graupius against the Roman legions, will probably never be confirmed. While the uncertainty is frustrating it is not critical, for Hemingburgh gives a full description of the battle in a location which obviously lent itself to defence, a burn guarding the west and a smaller burn and wet ground lying to the south and south-east. Although Hemingburgh's account is written from the English standpoint this should not have affected his description of the topography. One thing is beyond doubt: the position adopted by Wallace at Falkirk was nothing like as strong as that at Stirling Bridge. It was more suitable for a fortified camp than a place where he could feel confident of meeting superior English forces. The wooden stakes, pointing outwards, which Wallace prepared to help break the force of cavalry charges, could not be expected to hold up heavy horsemen for long nor protect his spearmen from the full force of massed horsemen.

In time-honoured fashion immediately before the battle Wallace addressed his troops. The actual words ascribed to him were terse enough, far shorter than his message to the English leader at Stirling. They were, 'I have brought you to the ring: dance the best you can.'[7]

One wonders whether the words were spoken with pride, as Fergusson maintains, or whether Wallace, the master of the feint and surprise was acknowledging he had been persuaded to accept battle against his fighting instincts, probably as much by elements within his army as by the determined actions of the English.

The English were eager to start attacking but, because they had taken virtually no food during the latter part of the march, the king proposed distributing whatever rations they had to help prevent both men and horses becoming exhausted if the battle proved protracted. With the amount of energy used both in hand-to-hand fighting and by cavalry forays it seemed an eminently sensible suggestion. Yet there is also a suspicion that

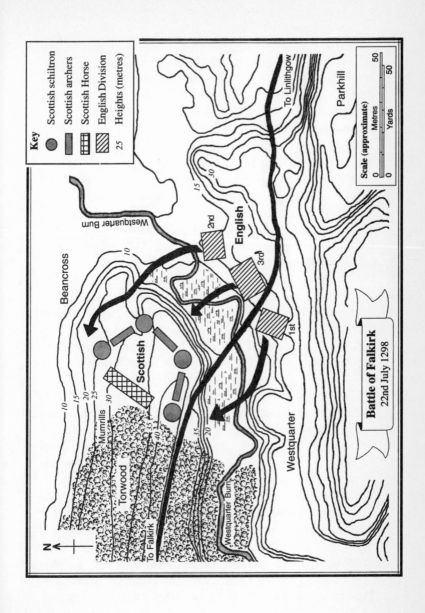

Battle of Falkirk
22nd July 1298

Key
- Scottish schiltron
- Scottish archers
- Scottish Horse
- English Division
- 25 Heights (metres)

Scottish

English

1st

2nd

3rd

Westquarter Burn

Westquarter Burn

Beancross

Mumrills

Torwood

Westquarter

Parkhill

To Linlithgow

To Falkirk

N

Scale (approximate)
Metres 0 — 50
Yards 0 — 50

10 15 20 25 30 35 40

owing to his injured ribs or even his age (like the rest of the army he had had virtually no sleep) he wanted a short breathing space. His officers, seeing the enemy on what appeared to be open ground with only a small stream as protection, opted for an immediate attack and seeing their enthusiasm the king gave his assent, and he ordered the Welsh infantry to begin the engagement. The Welsh, still smarting from their recent treatment, refused to move and it was the first division of cavalry led by Norfolk, the earl marshal, supported by the earls of Hereford and Lincoln, which rushed forward, only to find themselves impeded by a broad band of wet moss and, in their hunt for better ground, forced to veer westwards.

The second cavalry division now entered the fight, commanded by the bishop of Durham, a rather more thoughtful and deliberate fighter than the noble earls. He took an easterly route to seek out the Scottish left flank before ordering a halt until the army's third division, under the king himself, could join him and provide overwhelming strength. The proud barons under the bishop's command, no fewer than thirty-two bannerets and a trio of earls, chaffed at what they considered an unnecessary delay. Some were determined to attack immediately and one of them, Sir Ralph Basset, showed his boiling impatience by telling the bishop to go off and celebrate mass and let them concentrate on the fighting. As a result while the first division was still circling the Scots right-hand schiltron, and before the king had joined the battle, the bishop of Durham's division started attacking on the left. Such simultaneous clashes were the worst option for the Scots.

Despite the terrifying sight of armoured knights astride their heavy shire horses thundering towards them and the very impact made by upwards of two tons of man and horse crashing into the schiltrons, the spearmen stood firm and many horses were transfixed on their spear wall. Afterwards claims were made against the English exchequer for over 100 cavalry horses lost in battle. Wisely the English did not persist in such suicidal attempts and the majority of both horses and their riders remained unscathed. They had no need, for elsewhere things were already moving in their favour. The spectacle of the heavy English cavalry crashing into the spear walls was too much for the small detachment of Scottish cavalry who withdrew from the battlefield and, whether they knew it or not, the spearmen were already doomed. With no cavalry to oppose them the English were able to ride down the short bowmen whom Wallace had made responsible for covering the intervals betweeen the schiltrons. No one could accuse these men of shirking their duties for they and their commander, Sir John Stewart, displayed the utmost gallantry and, according to Hemingburgh, bodies 'of handsome form and tall stature' were found lying in lines around their slain leader. The Scots schiltrons now found themselves heavily besieged not only from their outer flanks but by cavalry which penetrated the corridors between the spear circles. None the less, despite the absence of bowmen and the withdrawal of their own cavalry, they remained unsubdued.

The crucial moment of the battle arrived with the entry of the third English battle division under the king. On his command their archers, who were able to keep a tight formation, released a deadly shower of arrows onto each packed schiltron in turn which, lacking both body armour and shields, had no protection against such indirect attacks. When their arrows had been expended the archers picked up round flints lying in the Westquarter Burn or scattered on the hillside. By means of slings or with their bare hands they hurled them from the shortest range upon the embattled spearmen who, with marauding cavalry all around them, had no option but to hold their positions. Many men went down as the assorted projectiles found their mark and, with the thinning of the schiltrons' ranks, further massed charges by the cavalry were at last succeeding in breaking the spear circles. From now onwards the slaughter of the Scots began.

Equally serious, by working his cavalry division around

the Scottish rear the canny bishop of Durham cut off their line of flight. It was his cavalry charge from higher ground which made the destruction of the Scottish forces inevitable. In the case of the common spearmen there was no question of mercy. With the outcome certain, Welsh daggers now joined in the carnage which marked the climax of what had been a relatively protracted but brutal conflict. About a third of the Scots army fled into whatever cover they could find and Wallace was still able to turn savagely on his pursuers when they came up with him in Callendar Wood. But in a rerun of Stirling the year before many of these were caught by the English cavalry as they attempted to cross the wide river Carron with its treacherous, muddy banks. Wallace had lost his main army and (however unfairly when one considers the behaviour of the Scottish cavalry) his own military reputation was diminished permanently.

Despite Hemingburgh's account of the battle, many questions about Wallace's own performance remain unanswered. On the one hand, to his immense credit, he had the foresight to adopt the schiltron formation against the English cavalry and the strength of will to impose it on Scottish soldiers who prior to this – often to their great cost – had invariably favoured offensive action. Whether on the day of battle he created an opportunity to maximise its great strengths is far more doubtful. As an army expressly designed to counter cavalry, its massed ranks would always be vulnerable to missiles launched from opposing formations and it had, therefore, to be guarded against such a threat. Although Wallace stationed bowmen to keep the English foot-soldiers at a distance, they were not numerous enough and their weapons were much inferior to their English counterparts. And was it not puzzling that he gave the vital task of protecting his bowmen to the cavalry, who were not only markedly unequal to the English mounted arm but of unproven loyalty? Why he did so, when he seemed to have such little respect for, or confidence in, his cavalry, over whom he never exercised full control, verges on the inexplicable. Perhaps he thought that by giving them such responsibility they would be forced to remain true.

On the other hand, despite the tactical problems of Falkirk, he might have come to the conclusion that such arrangements were the best he could achieve in the circumstances, and that low English morale, together with their physical weaknesses through lack of food, would counter-balance his lack of mounted men. Yet of all their arms, the English would have been most likely to keep their cavalry in good order. Even if the Scottish cavalry had fought with much greater distinction than Wallace could ever have expected, it was still outnumbered by at least six to one and must surely have been defeated, in which case the outcome would have been similar. The question why, given his weaknesses in both cavalry and archers, Wallace did not insist on his schiltrons being drilled to move from defence to attack is also worth asking. The gentle forward slopes of Falkirk certainly appeared to have made this possible. The shortness of the interval between his military foray into England during the winter and his next year's campaign might well have prevented him from insisting they were so trained, but did he think of it? We can, of course, never be sure.

What we do know is that Wallace's task at Falkirk was immeasurably more difficult than his and Moray's at Stirling Bridge. In spite of the odds he offered battle in circumstances which led to a heavy defeat and, however great a part the unexpected might have played, no commander can ever absolve himself from such a responsibility. The unrealistic task which Wallace gave his cavalry at Falkirk contributed markedly to his crushing defeat. If they had been held back to block the English cavalry from sweeping round his rear his troops would still have suffered a severe mauling, but he might have kept some sort of army in being, particularly since the starving condition of both the English troops and their horses ruled out any lengthy pursuit.

Finally, is there not a doubt, at least, about Wallace's control and leadership as overall commander during the battle? His opponent, Edward, on seeing his cavalry checked knew well enough that he must bring his foot-soldiers, including his archers, into the battle, and these tactics led to his eventual success. In the hour of test was Wallace prepared to amend his tactics during the battle? Might he even have been more stern than inspirational? When Julius Caesar, for example, met with disasters on the battlefield he had an astonishing ability to seize hold of a desperate situation and 'through sheer force of will and faith in his own genius transmute what to a normally able general would have been certain defeat into victory.'[8] In such circumstances Caesar always showed himself to his men and led by example.

After Wallace's cavalry fled the field we can only wonder at his possible reactions. As his hopes of victory died did he, in disgust or despair, temporarily detach himself from the action or did he always keep himself apart? A nineteenth-century memorial placed in Falkirk's public park at Lochgreen Road bears the inscription *Hic Stetit* 11 *die Augusti AD* 1298. Plainly the site of the memorial is inaccurate, but is the tradition behind it less so? Did Wallace watch the action from an adjoining hill in order to make more sense of its confused ebb and flow? Wallace's friends and fellow commanders, Sir John Stewart, Sir John Graham and MacDuff of Fife, each showed a soldier's example and died in the company of their men. A great rather than good general would, like Caesar, have retained the option of offensive action. Could not Wallace, whose bravery was never in question, have put himself at the head of a schiltron and led it in an attempt to break out, however risky such an endeavour might have been, even if it had not been fully trained for the purpose? At Falkirk was he more a spectator than he should have been? A chronicler unfailingly sympathetic to Wallace hinted it might have been so when, in the final stages of the conflict, Walter Bower has him slipping away in sadness from the battle.[9]

Wallace might have believed it was important for him to

survive because without his example opposition to the English would probably falter and it was the future of Scotland which mattered more than his military reputation. Immediately after the battle, for instance, he still had sufficient energy and strategic vision to destroy Stirling and Perth, thus denying them to the English. The English might have won an important battle, but their troops were in a bad state and food supplies continued to be inadequate. Edward, well aware of Stirling's importance for future military campaigns, attempted to repair the walls and regarrison it. But elsewhere Scotland was an inimical wasteland for his army, with St Andrews deserted and Perth an inhospitable shell. He was obliged to retreat southwards where, to his anger, he found Ayr burned by Robert Bruce who had then fled into the hills. The English king had no option but to return to Carlisle and close the campaign. Scotland remained unsubdued and, more serious for Edward, the campaign of 1298 had tended to increase both its national spirit and hatred of the English. Wallace undoubtedly lost the battle of Falkirk – but Edward's military undertaking had failed. This he acknowledged when, on 26 September 1298, less than three weeks after reaching Carlisle, he issued a general summons to raise troops for another campaign the following year.

Edward's greatest gain from Falkirk was that it removed his opponent from the highest reaches of power. In his single-minded determination to unite Scotland against the English invaders Wallace had made enemies among his own countrymen, common and high born people alike. Many, less dedicated, while supporting his objectives were not sorry that Wallace had been humbled and they now looked to more traditional leaders to come forward. The same men were determined he would never regain his former position. Yet the battles of Stirling Bridge and Falkirk had a greater importance. They caused a proportion of ordinary Scots, including burgesses and clansmen from the Highlands and others from central Scotland, as well as the landless, outlaws and those dragooned by Wallace's nationwide summons, to demonstrate that in addition to nobles and their retinues they, too, had their due place in the community of the realm.

CHAPTER SIX

≈

THE BALANCE SHEET
MAY 1297 – JULY 1298

Stands Scotland where it did?
Shakespeare, *Macbeth*

AFTER FALKIRK, ALTHOUGH WALLACE had seven more years to live, he never regained the pinnacles of military and civilian authority although, by his continuing defiance and death, he was yet to make an immense symbolic contribution.

Symbolism aside, how can we gauge his practical achievements? Some champions of Robert Bruce might understandably wonder how Wallace's fourteen months can compare with Bruce's twenty-one year struggle, how militarily Wallace's single major victory, succeeded by a heavy defeat, can be likened to Bruce's many engagements culminating in his triumph at Bannockburn, or how Wallace's modest attempts at diplomacy can be measured against Bruce's long period of patient negotiations (between fighting) which, at Northampton in 1328, finally led the English to renounce their claims to the Scottish kingdom. But this is surely to miss the point, for without Wallace Bruce would not have had the same opportunities. Wallace's achievements were fundamental in first checking then delaying Edward I's attempts to end Scotland's separate identity. Without Wallace's fierce opposition, for instance, the English king would probably have succeeded in placing his own representatives within the Scottish church, which would effectively have prevented the coronation of Bruce as King of Scots.

In his determination to preserve his country Wallace had been prepared to cut across conventions, both feudal and knightly, and to adopt novel military formations. Although these measures ultimately proved inadequate against English military power, they granted Scotland a crucial remission from Edward's programme of conquest and pointed the way for the English to be defeated later. After Wallace's victory at Stirling Bridge in September 1297 almost seven years were to elapse before, in July 1304, Edward could again seize the heartland of Scotland. It was not until September of the following year that the English Parliament was able to issue his ordinance for the government of the conquered nation, where ultimate responsibility was to be removed from its own king to an appointee of the English throne.[1]

Following Wallace's first great battlefield success and up to his death eight years later, the desire for national independence not only survived but, due to the sufferings of the people from all classes, it became, if anything, more deep-seated. John of Fordun told how, after Wallace had assassinated Heselrig, recruits flocked to the young leader. Their coming was significant enough but the reasons for it equally so: unsurprisingly, John of Fordun cited Wallace as the focus of 'all those who were in bitterness of spirit and oppressed by the weight of slavery under the intolerable sovereignty of the English dominion'.[2] After Falkirk few districts would be without families mourning sons killed by English arrows or war-horses, while those who survived the battle could not fail to carry their hatred of the English with them. The field had been prepared and the crop sown for another to develop and harvest, someone who combined the credentials of kingship with the necessary personal qualities. In March 1306, within six months of Edward declaring the Scottish crown defunct and Wallace's death, Robert Bruce, the most powerful claimant to the Canmore succession, took the irrevocable step of being made king of Scots at Scone, and thus uniting his own dynastic interests with those of his country. However slim his prospects of success might have appeared at first, Bruce, an enthroned king and leader of such a powerful family, could always command the support of far more Scottish nobles than Wallace, the squire who rose to the heights of knight and Guardian. But even in this Wallace showed the way and in his selfless support of kingship reminded men where their duty lay. Geoffrey Barrow takes pains to explain that a contributory factor in explaining the seeming cowardice and ambivalence of many Scottish nobles during the short period of Wallace's leadership was the notable ease of Edward's conquest in 1296, while the occupation that followed was too superficial to bring the Scottish nobles into open revolt, even though they were scarcely resigned to English overlordship.[3] Whether or not the full extension of English power was apparent to many at this time, in reality the state of Scotland, with both its central and local government firmly in English hands, had become analagous with that of Wales, until William Wallace and Andrew Moray – both aware of the dangers – showed others how control could be won back by force of arms.

While lesser spirits had collaborated or chosen to ignore what was happening the two guerrilla leaders were in the field and as a result, even prior to Stirling Bridge, the English garrisons were so intent on defending themselves that the detailed process of anglicising the country could not proceed. With Stirling Bridge, English military domination was broken and Edward could not retrieve the situation until he reoccupied the country. Single battlefield successes, even such notable ones as Falkirk, could not achieve it on their own due to the level of resistance stimulated by Wallace and now conducted by higher-born men. The whole country had to be brought under English control before Edward's new political system could be instituted and, despite Falkirk, the English king was far from capable of regaining such control. Although he rebuilt Stirling Castle, the most important fortress in central Scotland, he was soon to lose it and over large areas of central and northern Scotland his writ was ignored. While Wallace, now much reduced in position, was about to depart on a diplomatic mission overseas, the two noble Guardians appointed in his place (Robert Bruce and John Comyn) continued his work by besieging the English garrison in Stirling, while the Scottish church, under the guidance of Wallace's appointee Bishop Lamberton, remained almost wholly opposed to the English.

As long as Scotland stayed unconquered the spirit of national identity could – and did – flourish, and a proportion of those Scottish nobles who had chosen earlier to accept Edward as their superior could begin to consider whether their loyalties to their own country might be equally or more important. It was not always a straightforward choice, for some would change sides more than once. In some families brothers, or even fathers and sons, had different loyalties and these could switch as the more ambitious of them attempted to keep pace with the shifts in power. Yet Wallace's actions had kept alive the Scottish alternative through his successful military initiatives, both in set-piece battles and through guerrilla activities. By his scorched-earth policy up to and after Falkirk, he showed how the country's geography could best be used to thwart the English. At Falkirk Wallace had created a new infantry formation to confront the mailed knights of England, and his heavy losses there had deepened the divide between the two nations.

Wallace's own uncompromising attitudes also served to produce a harder reaction from his enemies than in the earliest days of the independence wars. After Falkirk, despite his relative leniency in other cases, the English king forfeited the lands of certain nobles who had openly supported Wallace and allotted their estates to men loyal to himself, such as Guy Beauchamp, earl of Warwick, or Robert Touny. In this context according to the chronicler Rishanger, Edward was, in fact, proposing to distribute Scotland among his followers who (if single) were to marry only English women.[4] A more conciliatory policy such as that of 1296/7 might have served Edward's case better, but Wallace's own unyielding stance was guaranteed to arouse the enmity of the English king against those who supported him and by extension against the continuation of Scotland as a separate country.

While Falkirk led to Wallace's resignation as Scotland's sole Guardian, it compelled more senior nobles to assume their responsibilities and, with his example in mind, together with their own sense of self-esteem, they went on to organise the dogged resistance which became a feature of the period between Falkirk and Edward's triumph in 1304. Baliol, kept under close watch in England, could do nothing, but Wallace's departure forced two leading – and opposed – claimants for the Scottish throne, Robert Bruce, earl of Carrick and John Comyn, to become joint Guardians – although their mutual ill-feeling quickly came to make such an arrangement unworkable (even when William Lamberton was appointed to help keep peace between them). When Robert Bruce resigned he was replaced by Sir Ingelram Umfraville, a nobleman associated with the Comyn and Baliol faction, and this decided him never again to accept what, for him, could only be a temporary and unsatisfactory institution. Bruce's resignation, therefore, marked the start of that long and arduous journey whereby, after first joining the English king, he came to see where his true future lay by reason of the sacrifice made by Wallace and others. After meeting and defeating other Scottish contenders for the crown he would take up the struggle with England for acceptance of his regal title over a fully independent country. In the meanwhile the level of resistance already aroused now enabled Scots supporting the rival Baliol/Comyn faction to keep the English at bay during the first few years of the new century, and prevented Edward from regaining control of that arch symbol of defiance, Stirling Castle.

The fruits of Wallace's political initiatives would also play their part in delaying the English occupation. As a result of William Lamberton's intercessions during 1299, and the reactions they brought from the Pope and the French king, Edward was obliged to release John Baliol from custody into the Pope's protection, despite his earlier plans to remove Baliol from the political scene, together with the question of Scottish kingship. Following Baliol's release the Scots appointed Sir John Soulis as a single Guardian, who introduced a new seal of authority; on one side it had the name and title of King John and on the other that of himself. In this way Soulis felt he could preserve the continuity of Scottish kingship by sending out his directives in the name of King John with himself in the position of witness. It was, of course, merely an illusion of power which fooled nobody, but it enabled the concept of kingly authority to be kept alive.

On the English side, owing to quarrels with certain of the English barons and the grave difficulties of raising a powerful army, 1299 was not a year for Edward to be campaigning north of the border. Yet his determination to crush Scotland remained unabated and the following year he led a formidable army into Galloway. It was, in fact, as large as that which had defeated Wallace at Falkirk but it could not be assembled until July, relatively late in the campaigning season, and he was soon to experience many difficulties. As a result, the English king had to content himself with a single military success, the capture of Caerlaverock Castle, and by 24 August he decided to end the campaign. Except for their progress in the south of Scotland the English were still a long way from winning back the areas liberated by Wallace and Moray in 1296/7. Edward showed how dissatisfied he was with his latest campaign by wintering at Sweetheart Abbey, south of Dumfries, which offered him a convenient springboard for a projected assault early in the following year. These plans were also to meet with a serious setback from diplomatic actions originating with Wallace, although continued by others.

At Sweetheart Abbey Edward was joined by a travel-weary and highly nervous archbishop of Canterbury, Robert Winchelsey, who belatedly brought him a papal bull drawn up in June of the previous year. With it came a covering letter, *Scimus Fili*, drafted by the Pope on 27 June 1299 – the day before David Moray's consecration as bishop of Moray at Rome. (Apart from his close kinship with Andrew Moray and his sympathy for Moray's and Wallace's undertakings, David Moray would go on to play an important part in Bruce's own struggles against the English.) The Bull strongly chastised Edward over his treatment of Scotland: 'We in no wise doubt it to be contained in the book of your memory how from ancient times the Kingdom of Scotland pertained by full right . . . to the foresaid Roman Church and that, as we have understood, it was not feudally subject to your ancestors . . . nor is it so to you.'[5] The Pope ruled that if Edward claimed a right to the kingdom of Scotland he should send envoys to the papal court to present his case there. The king's rage swept over his archbishop – but there was no avoiding the embarrassment: a reply had to be made. Such a reply needed much thought – and time – even for a skilled litigant like himself. In the event he succeeded in stretching English claims to the Scottish kingdom back to Eli and the prophet Samuel! But such activity was hardly favourable for warlike operations and as a result of representations made to him by the French, Edward was obliged to grant the Scots a truce until May 1301. None of this, of course, changed his determination to 'lay the whole of Scotland waste from sea to sea and force its people into submission.'[6]

While Edward was engaged in drafting his reply, the Scots, including Wallace's protégé, William Lamberton, continued their own political initiatives. The English king learnt that about this time, or a little later, Bishop Lamberton had in his possession a letter from the French king containing the statement that 'there will be no peace between him and the King of England unless the Scots are included. The people are putting their faith in this and in the success which they hope will be obtained by Master Baldred, their spokesman at the court of Rome'.[7] Master Baldred Bisset, a graduate of Bologna, was the outstanding pleader on behalf of the Scots who went to the papal court during 1300-1. Two of the points he made there had especial force. One was to contradict Edward's claim to the throne on the grounds that 'My enemies the Scots have recently acknowledged that I am chief lord of Scotland by hereditary right by a decree of their entire nation.'[8] Bisset maintained that not once had the Scots as a nation recognised Edward's sovereignty, even when under duress. His second submission gave the lie to Edward's claim that he was in full possession of Scotland. Master Bisset was able to say that of the twelve dioceses of Scotland the English king did not have the complete possession of any. That Bisset could make such assertions was largely due to Wallace's own past actions.

With the expiry of the truce in May 1301, Edward resumed his military attacks. Once more the results were disappointing for, although he captured Bothwell Castle, he failed to destroy the Scots south-western stronghold, which had been his main objective two years before. Much credit here was due to the Scots leaders, Soulis and Umfraville, who repeated Wallace's tactics before Falkirk by refusing to be pinned down and by vigorously threatening the English supply lines. Edward wintered at Linlithgow in preparation for the coming year but on 26 January 1302 he agreed to another truce for nine months, again as a result of French initiatives.

It was therefore not until May 1303 that Edward was able to prepare for a full-scale invasion of Scotland. He had succeeded in making peace with France from which Scotland was excluded. It was seven years since his first seemingly facile invasion of Scotland and six years after Wallace had demonstrated by his military skills how difficult this task might prove to be. Six years, too, since the young soldier patriot in his role as sole Guardian had anticipated a new dawn for Scotland among the community of nations by taking steps to secure foreign support for the long-established northern kingdom. It was a period when, despite the factionalism inevitable through lack of a true king, other Guardians had carried through Wallace's policy with considerable skill and determination of their own.

By the summer of 1303, though, there seemed no gainsaying the English king. Having learned from his earlier difficulties, he organised a fleet of thirty ships to drop off supplies at convenient ports in the army's path north and carried pontoon bridges with him to support his crossing of the upper Forth. It was not always plain sailing, though. In February as the English vanguard of mounted knights (formed into three brigades) were carrying out a deep reconnaissance near Roslin they suffered a serious reverse. Surprised by a Scottish cavalry attack many were killed or captured, including their commander, Sir John Segrave, who was badly wounded. Segrave was shortly freed in a subsequent English attack. Yet the Scots were unable to withstand the main English army and Edward met serious resistance from only two strongpoints, Brechin and Stirling Castles. The first held out for forty days while Stirling, under its commander, Sir William Oliphant, did not surrender until the following year.

Once across the Forth Edward moved northwards taking Perth in June and reaching the Moray Firth by September. Although Wallace had again taken the field during this campaign it was probably as co-leader of irregulars who, based on the moors of Selkirk, were only capable of making destructive raids against medium-sized English units or military convoys. He might well have inspired the ambush of the English vanguard but overall control of the campaign was in the hands of Comyn, who, despite his less than distinguished role with the cavalry at Falkirk, would never have considered yielding seniority of command to Wallace, whatever his past military record. After their experiences at Falkirk it was unthinkable the two men should even be particularly close. In fact, so reduced was Wallace militarily that, when William Lamberton requested him to do all in his military power to aid the community of Scotland, he also felt the need to contribute part of his own revenues to help sustain Wallace and his followers. Rishanger referred to him at this time as the chief of the Scottish leaders, but his statement was based on

Wallace's past position rather than giving an accurate picture of the present.

After spending the winter of 1303/4 in another great Scottish abbey – this time it was Dunfermline – King Edward confidently looked forward to completing his military conquest in the coming spring. His main object was Stirling Castle, the last major stronghold to defy him, and this he started besieging in April. Having already demonstrated his overwhelming military superiority during the preceding winter, he adopted a diplomatic offensive by offering lenient terms to all those who would submit to him before 2 February 1304. (This closely resembled his tactics in Wales during 1284.) But the mailed fist was also evident for he ordered a powerful force to flush out Simon Fraser and William Wallace from their wooded hideouts at Happrew, to the immediate west of Peebles. This was jointly commanded by such experienced soldiers as Sir John Segrave (now recovered from his wounds), Sir Robert Clifford and Sir William Latimer, along with Robert Bruce. They were led to Wallace's lair by a man called John of Musselburgh who was given ten shillings by the king himself for his help. Wallace still managed to escape due to a late warning about the raid. At least one commentator has attributed this to Bruce. Apparently not strong enough to mount an effective ambush, Wallace suffered heavy casualties which he and his reduced force could ill afford. Virtually all the other Scottish leaders, seeing little alternative, made their peace. The negotiations were conducted by John Comyn in his capacity as Guardian but it was noticeable that his demeanour was less abject than John Baliol's when he had abdicated eight years before. The requests for the defeated were made 'on behalf of the community of Scotland' and Edward agreed to Comyn's conditions that the Scottish people should be protected 'in all their laws, usages, customs and liberties in every particular as they existed in the time of King Alexander III, unless there are laws to be amended in which case it should be done with the advice of King Edward and the advice and assent of the responsible men of the land.'[9]

What these words actually meant and what chances the responsible men of Scotland would have had if Edward had determined to amend these laws is impossible to forecast. Yet the terms were quite close to those agreed by the Treaty of Birgham fourteen years before and they reflected Edward's graciousness in what he saw as a complete victory, before embarking on the inevitable exploitation. In his position as Guardian, John Comyn was treated leniently and when the other defeated nobles made their homage to the king on 14 and 15 March 1304, their lands were quickly restored to them. Despite his recent entreaty to Wallace to fight Edward, William Lamberton quickly made his own peace and by May 1304 he had regained his temporalities. Even Edward's inveterate opponent Robert Wishart, bishop of Glasgow, made peace with the English king, although he was required to stay out of Scotland for two or three years on account of 'the great evils he has caused'. By early 1304 all the Scottish leaders, except for Fraser, Soulis and Wallace, had yielded and could only now await whatever arrangements would be made for the government and control of their defeated country.

In 1305 a contemporary observer might have been forgiven for thinking that Wallace's and Moray's efforts had been entirely in vain. Despite Wallace's successes paid for by loss of life, the destruction of land and property, the sacrifices of individuals – not only among the nobles but the common people as well – things seemed scarcely better than in 1296.

In fact, the time bought by William Wallace proved to be of the utmost significance. Without his rising and military achievements Scotland would most likely already have been anglicised like Wales. Its proud succession of kings would have ended with Edward's own sad candidate, John Baliol. Because of Wallace, Edward had to spend nine years scheming and campaigning, years which helped to weaken even his iron constitution and cost his treasury dear. By 1305 he had but two years to live before being obliged to hand over responsibility to a son, 'chicken-hearted and luckless in war', who by no means shared his single-mindedness about the conquest of Scotland and who, far from being expected to complete Edward's mission here, could only give the Scots hope of escaping English domination.

Even with Edward still on the throne the position had changed. Since 1297 the Scots had put up a lengthy and determined resistance and his annual invasions had caused him serious difficulties in addition to their crippling cost. Such factors convinced Edward that, although he had succeeded in taming the country militarily, it was politic to give the Scots' leaders some sense of sharing in their country's government. During the Lenten parliament of 1304 held at St Andrews, the king asked certain leaders to advise him on what he was for the last time to call the 'Kingdom of Scotland'. It was agreed there that ten Scottish representatives should attend the forthcoming English parliament to help draft a constitution, and in September an ordinance for the government of the land of Scotland was drawn up at Westminster. The country would come under the control of Edward's nephew, John of Brittany, as lieutenant and warden, but ten Scots and twenty-one Englishmen would meet to decide on the nature of the administration. The highest and most sensitive posts, particularly those in the south-east, were kept in English hands, although in central and northern Scotland the sheriffs and constables were, in the main, Scots. Only two premier castles were entrusted to Scotsmen, Stirling and Dumbarton. As in 1297 real power lay with three men, all English: the warden, chancellor and chamberlain. As in Wales at the end of the previous century, the laws of Scotland were to be reviewed in order to remove anything 'openly contrary to God and reason', although the changes actually made were relatively minor and Scots (loyal to Edward) were consulted about them.

Nothing could disguise the fact, however, that Scotland was a conquered country without a king (it was no longer even termed a kingdom), garrisoned by foreign troops and governed by the officials of an alien royal house. Yet bearing in mind the prevalent attitudes of the early fourteenth century, the stubborn and long resistance put up by the Scots meant that English rule did not sit nearly as heavily as it might have done.

None the less, who could doubt that the 'new' Edward was still the old savage Plantagenet, still vindictive and vengeful against determined men who dared stand against him? This was seen in his attitude towards Sir William Oliphant who continued his defence of Stirling Castle on behalf of the Scottish crown, symbolised by the Lion of Scotland, when the rest of the country had submitted. During his successful campaign of 1303 Edward had been quite content to ignore Stirling Castle. He could take it the following year when he had assembled his massive siege engines which, with the rough humour of the day, were given names like the Vicar, the Parson, the Belfry or even Tout-le-Monde. The siege whose outcome could never be in doubt would provide him with amusement and, with the exception of the rebel Wallace, mark his complete triumph over once-defiant Scotland. Permission was given for Queen Margaret and the ladies of the court to watch the siege's progress from convenient windows nearby.

On 22 April Edward began his bombardment using thirteen great siege engines whose counterweights were made from lead stripped from the church roofs of Dunblane and Perth. Their projectiles weighed as much as 300 pounds. As Edward settled down to the process of battering down the thick walls, Oliphant asked permission to talk with Sir John Soulis who had charged him to defend it. He made the request in order to find out whether he might be allowed to surrender or had to defend the castle to the last. Edward refused outright. While he was probably reluctant to miss the chance of using his siege weapons he also wanted revenge. He rejected Oliphant's request with the remark, 'If he thinks it will be better for him to defend the castle than yield it, he will see.'[10]

The garrison held out for three months defying every missile, including the explosive and incendiary ones launched against it, until starvation made Oliphant offer to surrender. Edward's temper could hardly have been improved by the fact that during the siege the castle's defenders had come near to wounding him. They had struck his armour with an arrow – without piercing it – and on another occasion a rock launched from the battlements had brought down his horse. This hardly excused his response. In the first instance he refused to accept their offer until he had taken a further day exercising the pride of his engines, the Warwolf, as they crouched among its battered walls. When the Warwolf had done its worst he still refused them honourable surrender. This was in spite of their bravery and the mercy shown by William Wallace to Sir Marmaduke Twenge after Stirling Bridge and again by the Scots to the castle's English garrison in 1299. He threatened them with hanging and disembowelling. Only after they had acted as abject penitents, and Queen Margaret had interceded on their behalf, did he relent and send the fifty or so survivors to English prisons. Sir William Oliphant's reward was to be confined in irons in the Tower of London.

It was only to be expected that Edward would be implacable towards William Wallace, for he knew well that but for this man's defiance and determined leadership he would surely have achieved his goal far sooner. With Scotland cowed and obedient he might have recruited relatively large numbers of ordinary Scots (natural soldiers) for service abroad – as he had attempted to do with many ordinary Welshmen – and might conceivably have been hailed as the warrior king of Europe. Now it was too late and the one who, while alive, still remained a potent symbol of Scottish national resistance must be degraded and removed. Wallace was excluded from the concessions offered to the supplicants: for him it had to be unconditional surrender. 'And as to Messire William de Waleys, it is agreed that he shall give himself up to the will and grace of our Lord the King as it shall seem good to him.'[11] The details of Wallace's activities after Falkirk and Edward's relentless pursuit of him feature in the next chapter. But it was at this point, when deserted by his fellow countrymen, with further military successes plainly beyond his reach and the utmost dangers before him, Wallace performed his second greatest service to his country – the example he gave to Robert Bruce to go on challenging the English for the control of Scotland.

Even as William Oliphant continued his vain defence of Stirling castle, and projectiles from Edward's great siege engines were looping their way against it, two men, Robert Bruce and William Lamberton, watched the scene with a distaste they must have had difficulty in disguising. Both had found it expedient to make terms with the English king but both must surely have looked forward to a time when Scotland would no longer be a practice range for the English toys of war. Moving to the adjoining abbey of Cambuskenneth they concluded a mutual bond of alliance 'against any persons whatever' and agreed they would not attempt 'any arduous business' without consulting the other. The price for either man reneging was a penalty of £10,000 – an immense fortune – to be paid into the general fund for the Crusades. In fact, the greater penalty was their likely punishment at the hands of the English, since the subject under consideration was the placing of Bruce on the Scottish throne.

The heroic contribution made by William Wallace towards Scottish independence during the fourteen months allotted him both by the English king and his own superior nobles must never be belittled, despite the claims of Bruce's champion, John Barbour. If during the next few years of increasing isolation and discomfort, with the likelihood of an unspeakable death always in prospect, he helped Robert Bruce to assume his own daunting responsibilities, this second period merits reappraisal.

CHAPTER SEVEN

≈

IN THE SHADOWS

I offer neither pay, nor quarters, nor provisions.
I offer hunger, thirst, forced marches, battles and
death. Let him who loves his country in his heart,
and not from the lips only, come with me.

Garibaldi

AFTER FALKIRK WALLACE'S ANGUISH began. For a short period he had stood pre-eminent, sole Guardian of his country, dauntless in his proclamations to the great nobles and lesser men alike, unchallengeable because of his battlefield success over the much-vaunted English forces. Defeat at Falkirk changed all that. As one Scottish writer has observed, 'No man has yet been able to serve his country and least of all when it happens to be our country without undergoing some crucifixion, nor can he choose the wood of his own cross.'[1] It might have been better for Wallace, the man, if he had been killed at Falkirk. After Falkirk, like King Lear, he might justly have turned against the God 'that would upon the rack of this tough world stretch him out longer'. Whether Wallace had, as Blind Harry maintains, lost his wife as well as his closest blood relatives, the two battlefields certainly deprived him of brave comrades such as Andrew Moray at Stirling Bridge and Sir John Stewart and Sir John Graham at Falkirk. Blind Harry has Wallace reciting Graham's many virtues, and popular reports suggest the two men were warm friends, too.

Wallace's loneliness and exclusion after Falkirk was not due solely to the loss of those near and dear. His constancy of purpose and refusal to compromise played their part. With his own complete commitment he must have had difficulty understanding those who were willing to temper their ideals for the sake of both their families and estates. Before the battle he had shown scant sympathy for ordinary men reluctant to leave their warm beds and take up their places in his schiltrons to face the plunging horses and mailed riders of the English cavalry along with their deadly Welsh bowmen.

His conduct of war was always destined to bring him enemies as well as friends. Faced with being outnumbered in any campaign against the English, Wallace used a scorched-earth policy to help reduce the odds, a device hitherto used by conquering armies to cow the local people. Indeed, after Falkirk one would hesitate to credit anyone but Wallace with the burning of Stirling and Perth, for to him their destruction would be the lesser evil compared with English domination. Shortly after Falkirk Bruce practised the same tactic at Ayr and burned its castle, but such actions were hardly understood by the less committed, especially when the results appeared to be not entirely successful.

Wallace was also likely to have suffered from some measure of self-regret. After tasting high leadership and demonstrating an appetite and rare ability for it, loss of power would never be easy for him to accept. The individual whom some saw as an overbearing zealot could only have kept his post as Guardian of all Scotland, directing the affairs of his noblest lords and lesser men alike, if he were considered irreplaceable. After Falkirk this was no longer the case. Shortly after the battle he would, in all probability, have been obliged to relinquish the Guardianship, although what little evidence there is points to him laying it down voluntarily, possibly in disgust at the lack of support from the nobles and their cavalry detachments. While Wallace's attitude to the English invaders was not likely to change, John of Fordun hints at Wallace's deep regret for the sufferings he brought upon his citizen foot-soldiers at Falkirk and suggests this, too, might have been a contributory factor in his decision. According to this chronicler, Wallace, 'choosing rather to be of lowly position along with the common folk than to be in command when that involved their ruin and heavy loss to the people, voluntarily gave up his office as Guardian not long after the battle of Falkirk beside the river Forth'.[2] Another Scottish chronicler, Wyntoun, gave virtually the same account, pointing out Wallace's consideration for 'the leal commons of Scotland'.[3]

While Wallace's unswerving patriotism is unchallenged, because of his failure on the battlefield of Falkirk some commentators are eager to see his faults and to view him as a near fanatical leader, lacking the flexibility of mind necessary for high office. We have the picture of a man defeated through lack of support leaving the whole sorry mess to others. But the range of his achievements during the short period when he was both military leader and Guardian are far too impressive for him to be dismissed in such a way, nor did his career end there.[4] It was hardly surprising he should feel despondent after Falkirk. In later years the Duke of Wellington broke down after his great victory at Waterloo when he learnt of the large numbers of his loyal followers who were killed or maimed there. In Wallace's case he had not only lost brave comrades but defeat meant the end of his high office and his hopes to check the English king. It did not cause any weakening in his regard for his native land. We have no reason to doubt that after Falkirk, whatever the extenuating circumstances, it was Wallace who realised that others must accept their due responsibilities. He also recognised the pressing need to enlist diplomatic support from Europe. Before Falkirk this would have been highly desirable; following the battle it was essential for the continued preservation of the country. Diplomatic pressure might even now induce Edward to accept the person of a Scottish king (who in Wallace's eyes was still the exiled John Baliol). For the time being his own best contribution might lie in helping to negotiate with other countries.

For a number of reasons it seemed to make good sense for Wallace to leave Scotland. His ally, William Lamberton, was

then in France trying to persuade the French king to support
the Scottish cause and he might well have suggested that
Wallace would be useful in a similar capacity, either in
France or elsewhere. Whatever the cause, in late August
1299 Wallace sailed for the Continent accompanied by
at least five companions. He might well have gone first
to Orkney or Norway (presumably to try and persuade
them to send military aid) before he reached the French
court.[5] This seems entirely reasonable for, when he was
captured in 1305, documents of safe conduct were found
on him issued both by King Haken of Norway and the
French king.

During his time abroad Wallace never took a leading
part in the negotiations with France and Rome which
continued until 1303. These were left to men with legal
training and less unyielding images, such as Lamberton
and Master Baldred Bisset (clerk and president of the bishop's
ordinary court at St Andrews). In 1301 Sir John Soulis
acted as chief envoy for the Scots delegation in Paris,
surrendering his role as sole Guardian in favour of John
Comyn of Badenoch to do so. Despite the English king's
eventual success in removing foreign objections to another
invasion of Scotland, these diplomatic initiatives undoubtedly succeeded in delaying him. Wallace himself was certainly at the French court for a time. It was a measure of the regard paid to him there (and Philip's antipa-
thy towards the English at that particular time) that on
7 November 1300 the French king gave him a letter of
authority for presentation to his French officials in Rome.
This asked them to assist Wallace in any appeal he might
make to the papal court against actions taken by the
English king over Scotland. The document read as follows:

> Philip by the Grace of God, King of the French, to my beloved
> and trusting agents appointed to the Court of Rome, greetings
> and love. We command you to request the Supreme Pontiff

to hold our beloved William Wallace of Scotland, Knight,
recommended to his favour in those matters of business that
he has to despatch with him.[6]

After Rome Wallace seems to have returned to the French
court, where he could have been in considerable danger
when Scottish initiatives were frustrated by the military
defeat of the French by the Flemings. This, together with
Edward's unceasing diplomatic efforts, led to proposals for
a new bond of friendship between England and France
which was sealed by Edward's marriage to Margaret, the
king's sister, together with that of the prince of Wales to
Philip's daughter, Isabella. As proof of Philip's sincerity to
Edward, he seemingly had Wallace put under close guard
at one time. The English chronicler Rishanger reported
that the French were ready to turn Wallace over but that
in a merciful gesture, Edward merely asked the French
king to retain him in France. Rishanger, however, was a
heavily biased source and, with English diplomacy in the
ascendant, Edward was hardly likely to have behaved in
such a way.

Whether in France, Rome or Norway Wallace's role
appeared to be an informal one (possibly more in his
capacity as a former Guardian than as an official envoy)
but in view of his appetite for action later commentators
have felt he must have been involved in some major negotiations. Gray, for instance, is convinced he would have
met the exiled king, John Baliol, at the Vatican, but there
is no evidence to support this. Geoffrey Barrow makes the
suggestion that he could conceivably have led a Scottish
delegation to Rome as a counterbalance to the powerful
English one there, but again there is no proof. During the
spring of 1301 we have clear evidence about the men who
were chiefly responsible for the impressive Scottish pleading,
namely Master William of Eaglesham, Master William Frere
and the best known of them all, Master Baldred Bisset.
Wallace's name did not feature here. While he could have

undoubtedly lent weight to the Scottish cause Wallace was not equipped for the intricate and formalised nature of the arguments, and as the English king's prime object of hate he might have been thought of as something of a liability.

Significantly Blind Harry, never slow in listing his achievements, did not credit Wallace with any diplomatic successes, although he has him wielding his sword in heroic adventures, including one on his sea journey to the Continent where he overcame a famous pirate, Thomas de Longueville, and later fighting with a Scottish contingent against the English in Gascony where they stormed a town.

> When Wallace's men had thus the entry won
> Full great slaughter again they have begun
> They saved none upon the Southeron side
> That weapons bore or harness in that tide[7]

Harry has Wallace going to France on two occasions, the first occurring before the battle of Falkirk, but so similar are the versions that they were probably one and the same. The likelihood of two clashes with pirates with similar denouements is difficult to believe. Despite the duplication there seems to be some substance in Harry's account, for he refers to John Blair's part in the fighting against pirates, along with the contribution of the former pirate Thomas de Longueville. "But Longovel helped this time and Master Blair. Thomas Gray was then priest to Wallace."[8] Harry's main intention was surely to accentuate the heroic qualities of his hero and his words cannot be taken as fact.

Whether Wallace made a number of crossings to France or not, he was probably out of Scotland for the better part of three years. When he returned permanently it was to exchange the elaborate rituals and splendid costumes of both the papal and French establishments for the hardship and spartan habits of the soldier's camp, where ambush and betrayal were constant hazards. While he had been away things in Scotland had changed for the worse. High hopes for diplomatic successes had all but died. The impressive pleading of the Scots before both the papal and French courts appeared to have been in vain. Not only had the French king made his peace with England but the papacy had been much weakened by its quarrel with France. If this were not enough, on the domestic front the nationalist movement suffered a grave setback when Robert Bruce went over to Edward. It now seemed that nothing could prevent the English reconquering the country.

At this dire time it was hardly surprising that William Lamberton, Wallace's great friend and staunch nationalist, should turn to him to help stiffen military resistance. It was also utterly predictable that Wallace would not refuse such an appeal even if he was forced to operate in a much reduced capacity. William Lamberton's letter to Wallace beseeched him, 'for love of him and with his blessing, that he should with all his power give aid and counsel to the community of the said land of Scotland as he had done formerly'.[9] The letter also contained the telling offer (referred to earlier) of contributing a portion of his bishopric's income in support of Wallace's force, his band of irregulars (for they could be no more than that by this time). Without such an offer Wallace would have needed Comyn's support which, after that magnate's ambivalence at Falkirk, could scarcely have appealed to him.

Despite his strictly subordinate capacity it is unthinkable he would have lost his skill as a guerrilla fighter, and it could have been Wallace who conceived and helped to administer the sharp reverse suffered by Sir John Segrave and his cavalry at Roslin. If Wallace was present he must have been acting in a junior position to John Comyn or even to Simon Fraser. The pro-Wallace chronicler John of Fordun, who reported the action, would have left no doubt if

Wallace had been in overall charge. During June 1303, along with Comyn and Fraser, Wallace took part in an armed raid into Annandale and further south into Cumberland, although on too small a scale to make Edward divert troops from his own invasion. Nothing, it seemed, could stop the English king now, certainly not the minor detachments serving with Wallace. After English troops traversed the country, only Stirling Castle remained as a symbol of major resistance. The lenient terms of surrender offered by the English king – already mentioned – had brought the general submission of February 1304 and, apart from Sir William Oliphant (still in Stirling Castle), Sir John Soulis (who was to choose exile) and, of course, Wallace himself, all had made their peace with him.

After the fall of Stirling Castle the outstanding issue was the capture of Wallace and, given Edward's character, once he had succeeded, Wallace would suffer the ultimate punishment the king had devised for such men. Blind Harry had no doubt Edward desired revenge:

> To see him die Edward had more desire
> Than to be Lord of all the great Empires.[10]

The king had already shown how implacable he was towards Wallace in the previous year. During March 1303 Sir Alexander Abernethy, a Scottish leader who had gone over to the English, stood guarding the passages across the Forth when he became conscious that Wallace was apparently just south of him in his old lair, the forest of Selkirk. The somewhat naïve and nervous Abernethy asked the king what terms he should offer Wallace if he were to approach him with an offer to surrender. The king's reply offered no chance of misunderstanding, nor mercy: Wallace was no longer a defiant individual, he represented the last flame of Scottish resistance which must be extinguished: 'Know that it is not at all our pleasure that you hold out any word of peace to him, or to any other of his company, unless they place themselves absolutely and in all things at our will without any reservation whatsoever.'[11]

With the surrender of the other Scottish leaders early in 1304, Wallace's problems increased greatly. He was now their enemy; not only did they know his way of fighting but they knew his stamping grounds, including his 'safe houses'. Edward's mailed hand was at his very shoulder. As we know, in February 1304 the well-mounted force under the English commanders Segrave, Clifford and Latimer (joined later by Bruce), which mounted a surprise attack on Wallace and Fraser near Peebles, acted on information given by Scots. It is possible that Bruce – by far the most able of the commanders – could have trapped both men if he had wanted, but within four months he would enter into his secret compact with William Lamberton. If, in fact, he was following this devious path the risks were considerable, although at the time he succeeded in convincing Edward he was doing his very best, for the king wrote a letter to 'his loyal and faithful' supporter about the operation – and Wallace's elusiveness – which contained the words, 'As the cloke has been well made make the hood also.'[12] By March Bruce received news of his brother's death and, probably to his great relief, ended his part in the chase when he moved back into England to settle his family affairs there.

Edward tried to capture Wallace by putting pressure on other men who knew his ways. When James the Steward (Wallace's feudal superior), Sir Ingelram Umfraville and Sir John Soulis surrendered, their letters of safe conduct were made conditional upon Wallace's surrender. Umfraville and the Steward were never implicated in Wallace's capture, while it was Sir John Soulis' rejection of the king's conditions which decided him to accept banishment. Comyn was also pressured but refused to become involved. On the other hand none of them had the courage, nor even the interest, to speak up for Wallace and try – in the admittedly vain hope – to deflect the king from his revenge.

With lesser men Edward tried monetary bribes, offering £100 to any who would deliver Wallace to him. On 28 February 1305 he ordered the freeing of Ralph Haliburton to help in Wallace's capture (together with others from the garrison of Stirling Castle confined in England), but these incentives also appeared to come to nothing. By the summer of 1305, after Simon Fraser had surrendered to the English king, Wallace was alone and life must have been exceedingly difficult for him and those still with him. But Wallace's discipline held; he tried to keep his men as active as possible, although any foray was by now very dangerous. The last known skirmish mounted by them below Earnside occurred in September 1304.

One feels bound to ask why Wallace continued to hold out as he did when all other men of substance had made their peace with Edward and English power seemed unstoppable. While he could expect no mercy from the English king, there seemed no chance either that his band of fugitives could achieve anything worthwhile. The obvious option was to seek safety overseas until the position changed; the Scandinavian countries would surely have given him refuge. On the other hand, he might have received some verbal assurance from Robert Bruce that there was a major role for him in a new uprising for which Bruce was already taking cautious soundings. It is also conceivable that at the time of his capture, near Glasgow, he was contemplating a seaborne journey, either in the hope of finding other allies to support Scotland or just making his escape. Blind Harry (never a supporter of Bruce) suggests he was near Glasgow at Bruce's request and puts forward a different, and surprising, possibility, that Wallace might have been contemplating joining the Church:

> Thus Wallace thrice has made all Scotland free
> Then he desired in lasting peace to be
> For as of war he was in some part irk
> He purposed then to serve God and the Kirk.[13]

It will never be known why Wallace was near Glasgow. Perhaps with so many of his countrymen deserting him, even his burning patriotism had turned into some form of disillusionment and this might have made him careless about his personal safety. Perhaps after being hunted for so long he was exhausted and, lacking money and resources, was a fair prey for a determined hunter.

Wallace's capture came on 3 August 1305 and the man responsible was Sir John Menteith, a Scot who made his peace with Edward in March 1304. He was, in fact, the uncle of Sir John Stewart who had been killed at Falkirk and might have held this against Wallace. Edward rewarded Menteith by granting him the sheriffdom of Dumbarton and making him keeper of its castle. While Menteith could be seen as doing his duty to his current master, Blind Harry sees him as an out-and-out traitor, especially as Wallace had been godfather to two of his children:

> For covetise Monteith upon false ways
> Betrayed Wallace that was his gossip twice.[14]

It is interesting that both John of Fordun and the Lanercost chronicler agree with Harry's low interpretation of Menteith. Harry also tried to suggest that Bruce might have had some indirect involvement.

The act of betrayal is put down to one of Wallace's servants, with the unlikely name of Jack Short, whose brother Wallace was reported to have killed but who might equally well have been planted into Wallace's camp. Forty merks (equivalent to £30) were given to the servant for spying him out and a further sixty merks (£40) to others 'who were at the taking of the said Wallace, to be shared among them'. Blind Harry is understandably enraged and has the highest fears for both his hero and his native land.

> Alas Scotland to whom shall ye complain
> Alas from pain who shall thee now refrain
> Alas thy help is falsely brought to ground

> Thy best chieftain in breath in bands is bound
> Alas thou hast lost now thy guide of light
> Alas who shall defend thee in thy right
> Alas thy pain approaches wonder near
> With sorrow soon thou must be set a fear.[15]

Menteith made directly for the Solway Firth avoiding townships whose citizens might try to release his captive. Here he handed over Wallace to Sir Aymer de Valence and Sir Robert de Clifford who took him south to Carlisle, where he was secured for the night in the castle; the tower where he lay ever since being known as Wallace's Tower. At last Edward had him tight, although there was a 300 mile journey before he could parade his prisoner in front of the citizens of London.

CHAPTER EIGHT

≈

THE HERO'S REWARD

'Faithful unto death'
New Testament, Revelations

A T CARLISLE WALLACE WAS delivered into the hands of
Sir John Segrave who had been charged by Edward to
bring him safely to London. The two had some acquaintance.
Segrave might well have clashed with Wallace when Segrave
was wounded in the Scottish attack at Roslin and the next year
when he helped to inflict the defeat which Wallace and Simon
Fraser suffered near Peebles. In the hot summer weather the
journey southwards must have been arduous. It took seventeen
days and during the long hours spent in the saddle the prisoner
must have considered how every pace took him further from his
native land and closer to his terrible enemy. As for Segrave, who
could have had no illusions about his own fate if anything went
wrong, his whole concern would rightly be on getting Wallace
safely to London. Assuredly the prisoner was securely bound
whilst on horseback and both tethered and watched over at
all times during halts: in Blind Harry's words, 'secured with
iron chains that were both stark and keen'.[1] Such close security
would have made the journey more uncomfortable still.

On Wallace's arrival in London the Wallace papers suggest
he probably met with the king, if only briefly, who, whether
from guilt or contempt, apparently would not look at him
before sending him for trial.[2] James Fergusson cannot resist
taking the former interpretation, wondering whether Edward
turned away from Wallace in the same way that Argyll, looking
down from the window of Moray House, turned away from the
steady gaze of the captive Montrose whom he had betrayed.

Judging from Edward's prevailing attitude to Wallace, one can hardly believe that guilt would have made him refuse a meeting or that he would have inclined towards penitence rather than triumph: here was a man who had long thwarted his grand design and refused to be impressed either by his great office or his feudal seniority in the affairs of Scotland.

The word trial is hardly apt for what was to occur in Westminster Hall. As soon as Edward learnt Wallace had been taken, he made preparations for his execution. The 'trial' was a showpiece event designed as a powerful deterrent to others but above all it represented Edward's revenge against an inveterate and difficult enemy. Unlike other events in Wallace's life about which there is but imperfect knowledge, a detailed account of his trial was made by an eye-witness.[3]

On Sunday 22 August the prisoner entered London and passed through streets filled with curious, catcalling people, anxious to catch sight of the Scottish outlaw whose infamies had been related to them by their chroniclers. As a deliberate humiliation he was not lodged in the Tower of London, a privilege warranted by him as a former Guardian of Scotland, but was kept overnight at Fenchurch Street in the home of William de Leyne, an alderman and former sheriff of London.

On the next day no time was lost in proceeding with the mockery of a trial, although it was conducted with the utmost splendour and ostentation. Wallace was brought in procession to Westminster Hall through streets again lined with eager crowds. The retinue of notable men must have impressed the onlookers, moving as it did at a measured pace with the majority of its members, including Wallace and his escort, mounted on good horses. In addition to the cavalcade's commander, Sir John Segrave (now assisted by his brother) and Wallace himself, there was the mayor of London, together with those other senior officials appointed to sit in judgement over the prisoner, as well as sundry sheriffs and aldermen. Despite being denied lodgings in the Tower the wry thought might have occurred to Wallace that the procession was more appropriate for a king than a declared outlaw.

Once inside the majestic hall, its soaring hammer-beam roof and scarlet draperies redolent of English power, any hope must have disappeared as Wallace was made to stand beside a large scaffold at its south end, placed there to remind him of his certain fate. Then, as a further humiliation, he had a crown of laurel placed on his head. This was justified 'since he had reportedly said in the past that he deserved to wear a crown in that hall'. In a religious age why the authorities should have approved such a parallel with Christ's crown of thorns seems scarcely credible, especially for a man who had never sought the kingship of his own country.

King Edward took no chances over any technical flaws occurring in the conduct of the trial. The commissioners appointed were both eminent and highly experienced. The principal figure was the king's chief justiciar, Peter Mallore, whose senior co-judge was the constable of the Tower of London, Ralph de Sandwych. They were to be assisted by the mayor of London, John le Blunt; a commissioner, John de Bacwell; and Sir John Segrave himself.

Wallace was tried both as an outlaw and traitor. Edward, that master of the law, made sure that both the ritual of the trial and the sentence arrived at satisfied contemporary legal practices. Although, as an outlaw Wallace was not entitled to a trial, by bringing it the king could publicise his crimes and make a terrible example of him. The trial had just two stages, the reading of the indictment and the sentence, to follow immediately as the prisoner had no rights to dispute or plead against it.

The indictment was lengthy and highly damning; the chief justiciar made sure that no one in the hall could be left in any doubt about the prisoner's many and flagrant crimes which, even taken singly, merited a terrible death under Edward's system of legal jurisdiction. Wallace was charged with rebellion, sedition, homicide, robbery, arson, sacrilege and other felonies, including the slaying of the sheriff of Lanark and raiding the English border counties. The indictment took care also to call Wallace obdurate in that he had refused to come to the peace of his said lord, the king of England. This was, of course, not strictly accurate for Wallace had not refused to come back into the king's peace as he had never sworn an oath of loyalty to him. Despite having no right to plead on his own behalf, Wallace succeeded in saying a few short words, denying he had ever been a traitor to the king of England – having never pledged his allegiance. He acknowledged the accuracy of the other accusations relating to his actions during military campaigns, both as an irregular and as commander of the Scottish forces. There was no point in denying them and, in any case, he was not ashamed to have acted as he did.

Immediately after the indictment the Wallace Documents have Sir John Segrave read the sentence of the court and the horrible punishments, detail by detail:

> And that for the robberies, homicides and felonies he committed in the realm of England and in the land of Scotland to be there hanged and afterwards taken down from the gallows. And inasmuch as he was an outlaw, and was not afterwards restored to the peace of the Lord King, he be decollated while he yet lives . . . before being decapitated . . . and that thereafter, for the measureless turpitude of his deeds towards God and Holy church, in burning down churches . . . the heart, the liver, the lungs and all the internal organs of William's body, whence such perverted thoughts proceeded be removed out of his person and cast into fire and burnt. Furthermore and finally, that inasmuch as it was not only against the Lord King himself, but against the whole community of England and of Scotland . . . the body of the said William be cut up and divided into four parts; and that the head, so cut off, be set up on London Bridge, in the sight of such as pass by, whether by land or by water, and that one quarter be hung on a gibbet at Newcastle upon Tyne, another quarter at Berwick, a third quarter at Stirling, and the fourth at St Johnstone (Perth) as a warning and a deterrent to all that pass by and behold them.

The punishment was proceeded with straight away. Wallace was pinioned face downwards on a hurdle suspended behind two horses' tails in preparation for his journey to the Elms at Smithfield. The five-mile route was a circuitous one, taking in both the Tower of London and Aldgate to let as many onlookers as possible witness his humiliation. On this final journey he must have been cruelly bumped and jolted as he was dragged along the filthy and uneven streets, and subjected to the jeers and spittle of the bystanders. At times he must have been more than half-dazed but nothing could have stopped his apprehension over the infamies which his stalwart body would shortly endure.

At journey's end he was brought to another very high gallows where, to the satisfaction of the English chronicler, Matthew of Westminster, 'He was hung in a noose, and afterwards let down half-living; next his genitals were cut off and his bowels torn out and burnt on a fire; then and not till then his head was cut off and his trunk cut into four pieces.'[4] Blind Harry would have us believe that in defiance of the king's orders the archbishop of Canterbury heard his confession and enabled Wallace to take courage by gazing on his own psalter.

> He gart a priest it open before him hold
> While they to him had done all that they would.[5]

No other contemporary sources confirmed this heroic interpretation. Yet whatever doubts others might have about the details of Blind Harry's account few would dispute his final observation about Wallace's end:

> Right sooth it is, a martyr Wallace was.[6]

Wallace's refusal to temper his beliefs in the face of great personal dangers from both within and outside Scotland, and his hideous death as a result, gave Robert Bruce and the Scottish people a precept for their own national aspirations. In later centuries, at times of bewilderment and crisis, men have been able to turn to that early champion who had no such doubts, and in their impressionable years successive generations of young Scots have gained inspiration from his example. Just as England's patron saint, St George is far less significant to most of his countrymen than Nelsonian or even Churchillian virtues, so to most Scots the shadowy figure of St Andrew can hardly stand comparison with their great national champions, William Wallace and Robert Bruce.

CHAPTER NINE

≈

WALLACE AND BRUCE

'The bright face of danger'

R. L. Stevenson, Across the Plains (1892)

WHILE EDWARD'S ATTITUDE TO Sir William Oliphant and the defenders of Stirling Castle was the likely touchpaper for Robert Bruce's and Bishop William Lamberton's mutual compact to liberate Scotland and for Bruce to go on and become king, the example set by another man was far more influential

As Bruce contemplated the huge problems facing him, both from other factions within Scotland and in the person of an implacable English king, he was able to take encouragement from Wallace's outstanding achievements both as Guardian and military commander, together with his selflessness and continuing defiance during the last part of his life. Such personal example aside Wallace could have had a direct influence on Bruce. The evidence will never be more than tenuous, but three of the most careful authorities, Barrow, Fergusson and Mackay, suggest it could have been Robert Bruce, earl of Carrick, who knighted Wallace in recognition of his great achievements: the young Bruce certainly confirmed Wallace's Guardianship and when he became co-Guardian with Comyn he supported Wallace's earlier decision to instal Alexander Scrymgeour as royal standard bearer and constable of Dundee Castle. Bruce later referred to the original gift as being granted by Lord William Wallace which, as Fergusson reminds us, was the usual style given to a baron or landowner.[1] Wallace was, of course, neither of these and whereas it could have been no more than a mistake by a clerk it is more likely to have been an indication of Bruce's high regard for him. There is also a strong probability that he gave Wallace some measure of practical help by contributing a portion of the Scottish cavalry which accompanied his army at Falkirk. After Wallace's return to Scotland they could well have made plans to work together at a later date.

No one can pretend that in his earlier days Bruce mirrored Wallace's constancy but this is not to say he was above admiring it. For instance, he had two powerful reasons for making peace with Edward. One was his inveterate opposition to the Baliol/Comyn faction and his dismay at the possibility of a Baliol heir becoming king. The other concerned his own dynasty: the question of marriage was highly important to him. Apart from personal affection, his choice of Elizabeth de Burgh, daughter of the earl of Ulster as his bride, cemented a powerful alliance between the two families – although it cannot be denied that the earl of Ulster happened to be one of Edward's firmest supporters.

While many in 1302 might have thought Bruce's return to the patriotic cause only the faintest of possibilities, for the observer it is difficult to believe he could have ignored for long the problems of his own country. He had witnessed the terrible consequences of foreign invasions upon Scotland (including his own Scottish estates); he had seen Wallace's great endeavours and failure due to a lack of support from senior magnates (like himself); he had experienced the limitations of the Guardianship (having acted as one) and could hardly avoid the conclusion that the Scottish people could regain their due freedom only under the leadership of a king. If so, what man had better claims than himself? If other men with no aspirations toward kingship such as Wallace, Lamberton, Andrew and David Moray, Umfraville and Soulis, together with others far less powerful – local priests, lairds, freeholders and burgesses – appeared to hold freedom so highly, why shouldn't he provide the lead?

During his conversation with Lamberton at Stirling, Bruce could have learned that Wallace had also despaired of the Baliol/Comyn leadership and was even then looking for an alternative. Whether this was so or not, Wallace had bought time for a greater representative to fight for Scottish independence and showed Bruce the way of sacrifice, demonstrating that qualities of persistence and determination were quite as necessary as worldly experience and diplomatic skills. Evan Barron suggests that the manner of Wallace's execution, of someone whom Robert Bruce considered as a potential ally for when he must show his own hand, was the main reason for the great gulf which developed between him and the English king in the latter half of 1305.[2] It is most unlikely that any documents taken from Wallace at the time of his capture would have connected Bruce directly with any nationalist activities that occurred after he made his pact with the English king in 1302 – Edward would surely have seized him if they had. But there is a good possibility that he may have made some earlier compact, particularly as Wallace's brother, Sir Malcolm, had been one of Bruce's retinue at that time. Whatever the reason, from then on Edward became suspicious of Bruce's continued loyalty. On Bruce's part, with Edward's treatment of Wallace before him, he could hardly doubt that Edward would never accept another Scottish king, however deserving his suit, and would do everything possible to prevent the question being reviewed when Edward's son, the prince of Wales, became king.

As he laid his future plans with Lamberton, Bruce was likely to have turned towards Wallace because only he showed the great qualities needed. While Wallace had supported Baliol as the inaugurated king he was hardly a natural member of the Baliol/Comyn camp. In any case, Baliol was utterly discredited, and to Bruce the other Comyns were hardly of the required stature for kingship, and the Guardianship, while an important temporary institution, could never provide the rallying point for an oppressed but still proud people. The country had to be brought back to its destined course and Robert Bruce, who would be forced to adopt the obsessiveness of Wallace, putting himself beyond the compromises and safe-seeking adopted by many other Scottish peers, could surely have done with help from Wallace.

After Wallace's terrible death in August 1305 and his own defiant enthronement at Scone the following March, it could hardly have been a surprise for Bruce to find he now faced the full wrath of the English king, marked by 'a new and deliberate policy of terrorizing the Scots into submission'.[3] Three of his brothers, Thomas, Neil and Alexander were executed, despite the latter being in holy orders, together with his brother-in-law Christopher Seton, while his two senior bishops, Lamberton and Wishart, were imprisoned in irons. Before Wishart was released eight years later he would be blind. The female side of the family did not escape either, and his wife, sister and daughter were all confined. He needed to respond with Wallace's qualities of obstinacy and unyielding resolution, and Wallace's military methods also came into their own again. In the relatively early stages of his campaign Bruce, like Wallace, used the woods and remote areas for survival, making sorties from them with all Wallace's bravura. At his climactic battle of Bannockburn he adopted Wallace's tactical formation of the schiltron – protected once more with bowmen – but he extended it by switching successfully from defence to attack. At Bannockburn, like Wallace at Stirling, he was able to compress the English force within natural features, this time between a steep gully and marshy burn, with the same result that the English were unable to use their superior forces. However, at Bannockburn the Scottish cavalry did not desert their king as they had deserted Wallace and they went on to take their full share in a victory which gave the Scots renewed possession of their country for the first time since Stirling Bridge.

As in many other cases of public vengeance, Edward's treatment of Wallace was to rebound on him. Whether Evan Barron is correct or not about it being the main reason for

Robert Bruce's final break with the English king, it must have helped him and others to realise the importance of their own patriotism and the attitude of the English where their country was concerned.

When Bruce ascended the throne of Scotland, pledging himself to free his country, the ordinary people of Scotland – those whose assistance Wallace had sought earlier – began rallying to his standard, despite his sacrilegious murder of the Red Comyn in 1306, his military weaknesses and the terrible risks entailed. On 15 May 1307 one of Edward's supporters wrote that Bruce 'never had the good will of . . . the people . . . so much with him as now'.[4]

Like all outstanding leaders Bruce developed his own methods but, during the long years of struggle before Scottish independence was re-acknowledged officially in 1328, there were clear indications of the extent of the debt he owed Wallace, the selfless trailblazer.

CHAPTER TEN

≈

WALLACE, THE LEGEND

How Wallace fought for Scotland, left the name of
   Wallace to be found, like a wild flower
All over his dear country, left the deeds of Wallace,
   like a family of ghosts,
To people the steep rocks and river banks
Her natural sanctuaries, with a local soul
Of independence and stern liberty.

William Wordsworth

WHATEVER EFFECT WALLACE'S DEATH might have had on others engaged in the patriotic war, there is little doubt his heroic qualities will always serve as a powerful symbol for Scotland as an independent country and for Scots fighting against whatever they perceive as unjust.

The great figure of King Robert Bruce can never, of course, be forgotten but, despite the skill and daring with which he conducted his long and arduous campaign, Bruce as king fought for his own interests, even if they could never be divorced from those of his country. Despite the great dangers, which were often increased by his own fearlessness, Bruce succeeded and was able to die in his bed surrounded by his office bearers, and loved ones, while afterwards, as befitted one of his eminence, his body was laid in the abbey church of Dunfermline. Following much hardship and endeavour Bruce, the king, rightly enjoyed some of the honour accruing from his great office.

Wallace's reward, on the other hand, with his torn and dismembered body displayed in four separate locations as a warning to other defiant souls and his head placed on London Bridge to give sport to the gulls, was very different.

Yet, in the context of Scotland's continuing need for struggle and sacrifice, the ritual death of Wallace seems the more fitting. In fact no other Scots leader at the time, perhaps no other Scots leader at any time – except James Graham, marquis of Montrose – has made such a deep and emotional impact on his countrymen. And Montrose's great deeds took place after the free union of the English and Scottish crowns. Yet both fought for the doctrine of sovereignty, which they recognised as the traditional and legal form of government for Scotland and the one best suited to protect the independence and happiness of ordinary Scots against the self-seeking of many others, including their own nobility. As Montrose wrote of his country 'it cannot subsist in a body composed of individualities'. Despite their selflessness and astonishing dedication, allied in Montrose's case with military genius, the flawed characters of their royal masters led them to lose their lives in a bloody and humiliating way. Yet in the process both gained respect for their ideals together with the continuing sympathy and affection of their countrymen.

At Falkirk Wallace was nobly supported by another Graham, his friend Sir John, who fought with great distinction, being killed there, before James the only son of the fourth earl, accompanied by just two followers, raised his standard at Tulliebelton almost four and a half centuries later.

Along with the parallels there are contrasts between Wallace and Montrose: Montrose fought for a Stewart whose main seat of power would always lie in England, whereas Wallace's support was for the king of an independent Scotland. The image of the visionary Montrose lacking in both resources and men, pitted against a crafty and worldly-wise Argyll supported by the majority of Scottish nobles, is one to move any Scottish reader[1] but it can never remove Wallace from his position as the archetype Scottish patriot – who also lacked help from many of the nobility.

It was not only his aims, more ambitious than those of Montrose, but the scale of his achievements that earn Wallace this distinction. With the exception of Bruce, no one from his own generation, even Andrew Moray, whose potential remains unproven, can stand comparison with him. Others might have suffered the same unspeakable fate but they arouse little interest today. Simon Fraser, for instance, his companion in arms who, after making peace with Edward I, rejoined Bruce and was, like Wallace, executed, is virtually forgotten. Wallace's own brother, John, was taken to London and put to death but he was only just another casualty in the bloody catalogue of incidents during the Anglo-Scottish wars of seven centuries ago. Plainly neither deserved the same recognition. Simon Fraser had compromised himself with the English king while Wallace's brother, although admirably consistent in his opposition to the English, never acted at Wallace's level. Better cases might be made for the guardians Sir Ingelram Umfraville and Sir John Soulis.

Umfraville was made a Guardian after Bruce resigned in 1299 on finding it impossible to work with Comyn; earlier he had acted as one of four Scottish representatives who succeeded in negotiating an alliance with France. With Comyn and Buchan he commanded a strong Scottish force raised to counter Edward's invasion of 1300 which succeeded in acquitting itself reasonably well, while during the following year a force under his and John Soulis's command burned Lochmaben, occupied at the time by the English. But Umfraville, whilst undoubtedly an able man, hardly displayed Wallace's unwavering commitment to the Scottish cause. He delayed coming out against Edward, for instance, until after Falkirk (where his help would have been invaluable) and by July 1304, together with virtually all the other magnates, had made his peace again with the English king. To his credit Umfraville would not be persuaded to accept Edward's offer of safe conduct in return for giving information about Wallace's whereabouts. Yet from now onwards his loyalty was to the English: he fought on their side in 1308 against Robert Bruce's brother, Edward, as he attempted to reconquer Galloway and against Bruce himself at Bannockburn, where he was captured. At Bannockburn Umfraville apparently advised Edward II to conduct a feigned withdrawal and after the battle Barbour says he counselled the king to negotiate a truce for the long term of thirteen years, so that the Scots freeholders should be given time to lose their warlike habits and the new generation would grow up untrained.[2] Such a man hardly deserves the right to stand comparison with William Wallace.

In the case of Soulis all the evidence points to him as a brave, energetic man but one who lacked Wallace's intelligence. The chronicler John of Fordun was particularly critical, calling him 'simple-minded and not firm enough', although Geoffrey Barrow contests this picture of him. Soulis 'came out' with many other prominent Scots after Falkirk. In 1299 he commanded the force which reduced Stirling Castle after Edward's small English garrison had virtually exhausted their food supply and were compelled to eat their horses. As mentioned already, in 1301 he joined with Umfraville in besieging and burning Lochmaben Castle and when Bruce resigned in the following year became Guardian before making his own peace with King Edward.

In his capacity as Guardian, Soulis was responsible for leading the Scottish embassy to the Pope which included as main pleaders Master Baldred Bisset and William of Eaglesham. After Falkirk, he was among those who surrendered to the English, but was refused safe conduct until William Wallace had been taken, and although the other magnates went through a show of co-operating nominally with the English king, Sir John was the only one to refuse Edward's conditions point blank. Instead he chose exile in France, where he soon died. In spite of his loyalty and determination, the important role he played as a middle-of-the-road candidate for Guardian, and his leadership of the Scottish delegation to France, he had little of Wallace's charisma or his qualities of leadership in battle.

Like Samson in Milton's 'Samson Agonistes', through the quality of his life's work and by the manner of his death,

Wallace 'heroically [hath] finished a life heroic' and it was not long before his countrymen came to realise that, in fact, he had been different, that both his resolution and sense of patriotism exceeded that of others. By 1419 Andrew Wyntoun was writing to this effect:

> In all England there was not then
> As William Wallace so true a man
> Whatever he did against their nation
> They made him ample provokation
> Nor to them sworn never was he
> To fellowship, faith or loyalty.[3]

Wyntoun also referred to earlier writings – other than the chronicles – in praise of Wallace:

> Of his good deeds and manhood
> Great accounts I heard say are made.[4]

While one might expect the jingoistic prior of a Scottish Monastery to speak highly of Wallace, the case of John Major, writing over 100 years later when he was principal regent of the University of Glasgow, is very different. He harboured serious reservations over the accuracy of Blind Harry's account and his *History of Greater Britain* compared the histories of both Scotland and England in a most balanced and impartial manner. He even showed himself an early advocate of union between the two countries, yet his final praise for Wallace was unstinted:

> Wise and prudent he was and marked throughout his life by a loftiness of aim which gives him a place, in my opinion, second to none in his day and generation.
>
> This Wallace, whom the common people with some of the nobles followed gladly, had a lofty spirit, and born as he was, of an un-illustrious home, he yet proved himself a better ruler, in the simple armour of his integrity, than any of those nobles would have been.[5]

Far more than Major's historical account, however (which by its nature attracted comparatively few readers), the romantic, surging, adventure story, written by Blind Harry some thirty years before served to spread the Wallace legend. Although its unashamedly partisan and heroic approach was hardly destined to appeal to Major there is no reason to believe it went against the widely accepted opinion of Wallace at the time of its writing. Second only in popularity to the Bible, it passed through more editions than any other Scottish publication until Burns and Scott came upon the scene.

With Robert Burns falling under the spell of Harry's story-telling, Wallace's renown received a powerful new impetus. Burns described his reactions thus:

> The first books I met with in my early years which I perused with pleasure were the lives of Hannibal and William Wallace. In those boyish days, I remember, in particular, being struck with that part of Wallace's history where these lines occur:
>
> > Syne to the Leglen Wood, when it was late
> > To make a silent and a safe retreat'[6]
>
> and as I explored every den and dell where I could suppose my heroic countryman to have sheltered, I recollect . . . that my heart glowed.[7]

By this time the story of Wallace's deeds narrated by Blind Harry had already moved and inspired many others and by the beginning of the eighteenth century (which, of course, opened with considerable popular opposition to the Act of Union between England and Scotland) the heroic Wallace was much acclaimed.

Later in the century it was Burns's own writings which played a considerable part in extending his fame. Just as his Ayrshire Scots language, often united with a Highland tune, made his words acceptable to all Scotsmen, so his admiration of Wallace – the great Lowland Scot – and his recognition of him as the father patriot of the whole country were carried by his writings across the English speaking world. Scots could believe that, if they had been in their ancestors' shoes, they would "hae wi' Wallace bled" and through Burns' own strong sense of nationalism and egalitarianism (despite his occasional display of Unionism) they could appreciate Wallace's disregard for earthly fame – "The rank is but the guinea's stamp, The man's the gowd for a' that." With Burns they could support Wallace's own contempt for falsehood and dishonesty. Above all Burns painted Wallace as the champion of Scotland's free voice.

> Where is that soul of freedom fled?
> Inmingled with the mighty dead
> Beneath the hallowed turf where Wallace lies
> Hear it not Wallace, in thy bed of death.

As a Lowlander it was natural for Burns to sympathise with someone like Wallace who, lacking the Celtic pretensions of Robert Bruce, could never act the swashbuckling part of Montrose when he donned 'Highland dress of trews, a short coat and a plaid for the shoulders . . .'[8] before joining up with his small army of Ulstermen and Gordon Highlanders. Burns understood, too, why Wallace could never become swashbuckling in the grander manner of the Stewart kings.

The powerful support of Blind Harry and Robert Burns might seem enough but, not to be outdone, Sir Walter Scott came to near veneration of Wallace in his *Tales of a Grandfather*: 'Sir William Wallace, that immortal supporter of the independence of his country, was no sooner deprived of his life, in the cruel and unjust manner I have told you, than other patriots arose to assert the cause of Scottish liberty.'[9]

Like other notable figures with high reputations, some of Wallace's biographers have inevitably pursued revisionist paths. Yet Wallace is not a particularly easy subject. While one can hardly expect important new material about him to surface after the best part of 700 years, the known facts underline his selflessness, and biographers are fully aware that Wallace's place in the hearts of his countrymen seems unassailable, whatever they might write.

While the Georgians or the Victorians were unlikely to take

a critical approach, later writers have adopted both strictly impartial and deliberately critical attitudes. The legend of Wallace, the courageous, surmounts them all. Despite his careful attempts to confine himself to verifiable sources and consciously avoid excessive praise, James Fergusson's excellent twentieth-century account ends with conclusions hardly less enthusiastic than those of earlier biographies and ones which certainly do nothing to lessen Wallace's reputation:

> An obscure man who became a great general, a brave, resourceful and tireless commander, an humane and generous foe . . . and a leader who won the trust and respect of his followers. Above all in his own time he was the only Scottish general of the war of independence who never submitted to England, never faltered in his loyalty to his king and countrymen and never despaired or wavered at the end.[10]

Writing in the late twentieth century, both James Mackay and Andrew Fisher, fully acknowledge Wallace's immense achievements but Fisher pays critical attention to his personal characteristics. Despite the savage context of his age, Fisher sees Wallace as a harsh man who did not help himself by browbeating others whose help was vital. Fisher questions the good sense of Wallace's support for the unfortunate Baliol and comes to the conclusion that, for Baliol to stand any chance of being restored, Wallace would have been compelled to reach some sort of arrangement with the English king. He leaves the suspicion – no more – that Wallace might even have had an alternative in mind, i.e. himself. If Wallace featured in this way his selfless patriotic stance was bound to be compromised. In spite of such criticisms and conjectures – for new evidence is not forthcoming – Fisher hardly dents the Wallace legend.

Of the modern writers, Geoffrey Barrow probes most deeply into the essentially tragic nature of Wallace's career due, in considerable part, to his Scottish attributes. Although Barrow fully acknowledges Wallace's ability to speak to ordinary men and, like other great leaders, to inspire them with a sense of common purpose 'to which they could not normally attain', he also sees him as a man of a conservative frame of mind. He was a leader who accepted uncritically his country's political structure with 'the community of the realm of Scotland, free and independent, owing allegiance only to its lawfully established king'. If the king was unable to act as leader the great magnates or senior church leaders had to act in the interim. If they failed then any responsible man must take up the task – as Wallace did from the time of Stirling Bridge onwards.[11] To Barrow, Wallace's tragedy lay in the fact that because Scotland was also conservative – even when engaged in a life-or-death struggle – it followed that, unless he could keep on displaying unimaginable military gifts, the country would turn again to a king or one of its great barons. Wallace, therefore, knew that his role could only be temporary. The unbroken battlefield successes which he needed were not possible because of the lack of support from the nobles and their horsemen. Barrow argues that after his defeat the rallying of the magnates towards their traditional responsibilities removed his *raison d'être*. From Falkirk onwards he was doomed to frustration and ultimate disgrace: even if the English king had not acted in the terrible way he did, jealous men within Scotland would never have let him reassert his earlier authority.

Despite the acuteness of such observations, particularly the age-old need of Scotland, as a land of diverse peoples with strong local traditions, for a unifying figure, they in no way destroy Wallace's stature. Indeed, the awareness Wallace had of his inevitable fate adds to it. For beyond all his other characteristics, Wallace represented an individual's self-effacing love for his native land which surpassed temporal concerns – including personal happiness – even life itself. That he acted in this way at the very beginning of the fourteenth century, when most of Europe was still feudal and the modern spirit of nationalism was just emerging, is exceptional.

In addition to such literary contributions about Wallace we have the comments of that cross-section of Victorian notables at the founding of his national monument at Stirling. In spite of their marked self-approval, those Victorians who gathered there saw him as an inspirational figure for all times and, more important still, for all true Scots. There was, of course, a strong element of these men seeing in him what they most believed in themselves, for instance the strength of religious influences on him, and his military accomplishments acting as a model for subsequent generations. They also approved his respect for education and his conservative attitude to the established political structure of his country. The entrepreneurs among them could even persuade themselves he was an early champion of Scottish free trade. But above all, in their eulogies these Empire-builders recognised his great personal qualities: energy, courage, single-mindedness, allied to an uncompromising belief in what he knew was right. He combined these with a contempt for time-servers, which appeared in no way to affect his faith in the dignity of man. Whether they were soldiers, administrators, churchmen or businessmen, and whether they came from the north or from Wallace's own region, all could convince themselves these were archetypal Scottish virtues, the very qualities that had already led Scots on to endless confrontations and many great achievements. Putting aside their own pride in material advances and individual wealth some might also have seen him as a tragic hostage to fate in a country whose geography gave it stormy seas on three sides and no great mountain range to guard its land boundary on the fourth.

Dedications to Wallace started long before the Victorians, and have by no means ceased with them. Scots of all persuasions have been accustomed over the years to turn to him both to help explain their history and to bolster their pride. Like young Robert Burns, many of the children who read about him today or watch videos dedicated to him will still find themselves awestruck by his fearless resolution. His comparative failure and unspeakable death have only served to enhance the legend.

The patriot idealist of 700 years ago, whose beliefs remain

untarnished, strikes a chord greater than that of others who achieved more: beyond the image of Robert Bruce and of other Scottish kings who had to struggle and compromise with the realities of power; beyond that of the tragic Stewarts whose story might still captivate Highland societies but whose memory can never again inflame them to action; beyond contemporary monarchs of both England and Scotland whose functions in the north are mostly confined to ceremony; and beyond the image of John Knox whose ironbound Calvinism no longer fits contemporary Scotland and whose pioneering work for education and relief of the poor has long passed into the hands of the state.

≈

CHAPTER ELEVEN

WALLACE AND
THE SCOTTISH NATION

Had Wallace fought for Greece of old
His urn had been of beaten gold:
The children of his native land
Had hewn for him, with cunning hand,
A mountain for a monument

J.M. Davidson, *Scotia Rediviva*

I**T IS DIFFICULT TO** gauge how far the achievements of Wallace (and other Scottish heroes) have contributed to the strong sense of collective pride and conscience which in later centuries propelled a small rural country into the forefront of industrial nations and led its countrymen to distinguish themselves on the world stage. But given the key elements of the Scottish temperament they could hardly have been insignificant. However, by the early part of the nineteenth century their names were being mentioned not only for their past achievements but with considerable frequency as role models for revisionism, for amid such economic progress there ran a sense of servitude and inequality.

Before the great Reform Bill, Scotland was impotent pol-itically and among its working people and the aristocracy alike, there was growing unease with the antiquated and quite inadequate system of Parliamentary representation. Burns was by no means alone in his enthusiasm for the ideals of liberty, equality and fraternity, and about the need for political reform. New newspapers, such as *The Scotsman* and *Ayr Advertiser*, were established to give voice to middle-class unease, while at radical rallies French revolutionary airs were sung together with Robert Burns's 'Scots wha' hae" featuring Wallace and Bruce. At this time the latter tune was felt to be so dangerous that Paisley magistrates considered making it an offence even to tap it out on a drum.[1] The growing tide of political agitation was checked – for the time being – when the Reform Act of 1832 broadened Scotland's national and local franchises.

Yet many Scots were quick to see that such a measure, constructive as it was, brought no immediate answers to particular Scottish problems, notably the difficulties arising from the sharp rise in urban population and the grim working conditions of many who contributed to the industrial boom. Across different levels of society a sense of outrage grew against suffering and injustice amid such rapid progress combined with the remembrance of traditional hard-won liberties. From the time of the Reform Act onwards attention came to be centred on questions affecting individuals, such as working practices and improving public health and housing, but in the later years of the century interest turned towards greater freedom for the country itself. What could be guaranteed was that once the imagination of Scots was captured by the need for reform, their polemical and logical tendencies were bound to produce dramatic and unsettling results.

The Kirk, which had always taken such a leading role in society, appeared to mirror the perceived need for change when in 1843 its evangelical wing reacted against the practice which had grown up of landowners appointing their own ministers. As a mark of their conviction that it was the right of male heads of families, to appoint or reject a presentee, 400 ministers ceremonially walked out of the General Assembly and declared themselves the Free Church of Scotland, despite the great personal and economic sacrifices involved.

If the Kirk could act in this way it was only a matter of time before equally strong reactions came from others including working men in protest against the suffering which many attributed to the headlong dash for industrialisation. The workers, no less than their clergymen and academics, showed themselves fearless in pursuing their arguments to the limit. While during the early part of the century much of the artisans' attention was taken up with broadening the franchise and support for the radical Chartist movement, as the century progressed and competition from other industrialised countries became keener their enthusiasm for unbridled capitalism cooled. Their goal did not stop at better working conditions: the working class, like their evangelical church ministers, wanted something more fundamental. With Scottish covenanting fervour they aspired to a country not only free from social and economic discrimination but one with far greater responsibility for its own affairs: the belated appointment of a Scottish secretary of state did little to satisfy such objectives.

The land that had earlier produced the economic doctrines of John Stuart Mill now became the birthplace for socialism as a political force. Yet in Scotland socialism had a patriotic face. The programme of the Scottish Labour Party came to include home rule, in addition to its traditional aims, such as nationalisation of both land and mineral resources, an eight-hour working day, state insurance against ill health and old age, abolition of the House of Lords and the disestablishment of the state churches. Due to nationalist currents in Scotland, and Gladstone's determination to give Ireland home rule, the Liberal Party, which was still far more powerful in Scotland than the socialist movement, also came to adopt the home rule platform.

Like the radicals in the 1820s who invoked the old champions of freedom so, in the twenty years or so before the First World War, those pressing for home rule or some further degree of national independence felt bound to cite William Wallace in their support. Writings on home rule during this decade included a monograph by J. Morrison Davidson, couched in colourful language and making free use of partisan arguments.[2] Unsurprisingly Wallace featured highly. To Davidson, Wallace represented the most powerful single source of inspiration (the others were George Buchanan,

Fletcher of Saltoun and Thomas Spence) against the repression and degradation of individual liberties since the Act of Union. Characteristically, he quoted Burns's picture of Wallace as the ever-continuing symbol of resistance:

> At Wallace' name, what Scottish blood
> But boils up in a springtime flood
> Oft have our fearless fathers strode by Wallace' side
> Still pressing onward, red-wat shod or glorious died.

Davidson selected Wallace not only as a man who fought ceaselessly for Scotland's freedom, but as someone who, in the initial stages of his campaign, had virtually no support from the often treacherous nobility and was utterly deserted by them at the end. Equally important to Davidson was the fact that Wallace enjoyed the support of the ordinary men of Scotland whom he aroused from their vassalage. He was not only a popular leader but a perfect hero image for socialists and radicals of all hues. 'In other words by the consent of the community this extraordinary outlaw not yet thirty years old is virtual President of a Scottish commonwealth with the hereditary feudal caste left out in the cold.'[3]

Davidson's document is notable in that, after nearly 600 years, the author felt Wallace's message could still provide inspiration for a nineteenth-century independence movement. Within the next decade, together with agitation for more and stronger departments of Scottish history in the universities, pressure mounted for further recognition of Wallace by way of another memorial, this time in his home town of Elderslie. In 1909 when the Scottish Patriotic Association, whose declared aim was 'to keep burning brightly the flame of Scottish patriotism', met at Elderslie their chairman, Mr George Eyre Todd, did not fail to remind his supporters that both Wallace and Burns were champions of Scotland, one for his deeds, the other for the songs that recounted them:

In that story [of Wallace] and in those songs lay the seed of all manly, upright and independent character, the character which in the past had made Scotland great and had made Scotsmen bulwarks of the world's strengths and pioneers of the world's progress.[4]

In August of the following year the Scottish Patriotic Association met for a second time to commemorate Wallace 'the maintainer of Scottish liberty' at the memorial cross raised to him at Robroyston. During his address their president, James McFarlane, a former bailie, referred publicly to political initiatives towards greater independence and the possible formation of a Scottish National Party in the House of Commons. As yet he seemed far from optimistic about its prospects, for he contented himself with the remark that 'if the people took it in hand they might make something of it'. Despite quoting Wallace's own unyielding example, at this time the overwhelming proportion of nationalists stopped at the goal of home rule.

During the next year it was the turn of the Wallace monument at Stirling to host a large gathering of his supporters, to celebrate the fiftieth anniversary of his national memorial there. In a re-run of the original ceremony attempts were made to see Wallace not only as the champion of independence but, paradoxically, as the statesman who would have approved the association between England and Scotland. The main address was given by the Revd Dr T.M. Robertson of St Ninians who declaimed, 'While Wallace was a brave and skilful man of war but [sic] he was also an earnest lover of peace and vision at home and, now the Great Britain – England and Scotland – had been so long and prosperously welded together, had not his ideas as a statesman been verified?'[5]

On 30 September 1911, with the unveiling of Wallace's memorial in Elderslie – made of Aberdeen granite to reflect the hero's immovable determination – a return was made to the theme of an independent Scotland and the value of Wallace's inspiration here. During the ceremony a pipe band played 'Scots, wha' hae', the tributes were highflowing, patriotic feelings ran high and at times facts were stretched to, or even beyond, the limit. Among them was an oration by a Colonel Greig who told the assembly that 'out of blood, tears and suffering Scotland was born ... The old feudal idea of our lordship had been rejected and nobles, gentry and peasantry became a united nation and with the victory at Stirling founded Scotland.' Oh, that historic events could ever be quite that straightforward!

Shortly after the outbreak of the First World War, a further gathering was held at Elderslie under the auspices of the Scottish Home Rule Association. Its flamboyant president, R. B. Cunninghame Graham, later to become first president of the Scottish National Party, left his supporters in no doubt about the relevance of Wallace and Bruce to its existence. The Association's purpose was to 'give voice to Scottish thought and conviction that the great work begun by Wallace and completed at Bannockburn by Robert Bruce must be further advanced by giving back to our country her own Parliament in Edinburgh for the advancement of all purely Scottish affairs.'[6]

Other moves towards independence were suspended during the conflict and, under the overall leadership of a Scottish soldier hardly less determined than Wallace, the costs of winning became agonisingly high. Scotland lost 10 per cent of its young men and this, together with the long-lived Depression afterwards, went far to sapping much of the nation's past confidence. As Agnes Mure Mackenzie put it so poignantly:

> In Scotland the end of the twenties had brought to ruin the structure which two hundred years before had risen valiantly out of ruin. Men looked upon a growing desolation where the hard won fields were turning again to muir and the emigrant ships were sailing down the Clyde between empty yards.[7]

From being more prosperous than much of England and Wales – in 1914 Scottish investments abroad averaged £110 per head of the population – by 1933 average wages in Scotland had fallen to some 14 per cent below those of the other two countries; the unemployment rates were higher and investment lower.

With such economic weaknesses home rule became a less attractive option for the political parties and the resurgent Labour Party which, after 1932, surpassed the Liberals, became more concerned with the social and economic crisis. Nevertheless, in 1928 the Scottish National Party was formed, with the aim 'to secure self-government [for Scotland] with independent national status within the British group of nations'. While Wallace (and Bruce) were still rallying points for Scots trying to escape their political bondage, during the 1920s the Labour Party supporters who made up the great majority of men gathered at Elderslie did so in the hope that his powerful image could give them increased heart to fight the economic troubles and the injustices suffered by working men, rather than gain home rule. In the 1930s Scottish communists on their marches against unemployment also carried placards of Wallace and Bruce alongside Marx to rally support. Although ordinary men and women no doubt continued to feel proud of their country and their race by reading about their heroes' successes during the revolutionary wars, they were now being held up as role models by some who, in virtual despair at the current economic system and the politicians who supported it, were committed to change it root and branch rather than to press for greater freedoms within it. For the majority, Wallace began to stand in some danger of becoming marginalised.

This trend continued during the Second World War when Douglas Young, dedicated pacifist, Aberdonian poet and chairman of the Scottish National Party, used the annual gathering at Elderslie to launch an attack not only on the conduct of the war but to ask whether or not it could be justified. His address contained the words, 'In this year of disgrace 1943 the chief political functionary in our Kingdom is the Secretary of State who is not subject to the authority of any Scots democratic assembly whatever.'[8] Young referred to an 'imperialist, biological war on the Scottish nation' and against it he cited Wallace as the best leader in olden days who succeeded because he aroused the whole people. The people should again be aroused to make Scotland a world of national democracy. His reference to biological war concerned the conscription of Scots girls to work in under-staffed English munitions factories. Young's particular ideas for a world of national democracy were never in the main tradition of Scottish political thought. At Elderslie in August 1944 the message from the new leader of the Scottish National Party, Dr Robert McIntyre, proposed an economy planned in every aspect, albeit within an independent Scotland. He heartened his supporters by telling them that 'six hundred years ago Wallace could have become a highly paid quisling but he was loyal to Scotland and refused to become such a person'.[9]

Scotland's losses in the Second World War were far less than in the previous one. At its close, along with the rest of Britain, the country looked out upon a world where the economic opportunities seemed unlimited. At the same time Scots helped to elect a Labour government at Westminster pledged to end the worst inequalities of the past and to devote much of its resources to giving a marked measure of security for all during sickness, unemployment and old age. To help avoid another war the country's external security became the responsibility of an alliance system of western democracies where British forces would take a full, if not a dominant, part.

In a Scotland where such major social changes were to be complemented by new international projects, both military and economic, Wallace's image might reasonably be expected to change, too.

≈

WALLACE
AND SCOTLAND TODAY

To 'fend our realm it is my debt by skill
Let God above reward me as he will

Blind Harry (Book 8)

I T IS HARDLY THE purpose of a book about Wallace and his
national legacy to spend undue time on the detailed political
occurrences of the last fifty years, or to forecast future patterns.
This is surely the province of others. What does stand out is
that during the last fifty years, the time and attention Scots
customarily spend on political questions, whether in the press,
television or radio, has been markedly different than in the
past, particularly during the first fifty years after union when
political questions were heavily muted. As many homeland
Scots find their involvement in industrial and commercial
concerns no longer so exclusive and see many of their most
pressing social issues satisfied through the machinery – albeit
increasingly dismantled – of the welfare state, their interest and
energies have turned once more to the nature of their political
environment. Being Scots they are tenacious in their analysis. In
this context notable developments have taken place. There has,
for instance, been a dramatic rise in the movements towards
greater independence.

During the early 1970s the subject was taken up briefly
by the Tory prime minister, Edward Heath, through his
devolution proposals which admittedly came to nothing after
his defeat and the election of Margaret Thatcher as party
leader. Towards the end of the decade Harold Wilson's own

devolution proposals (inherited by the short-lived and failing Callaghan ministry) were finally given the Royal Assent – subject to a referendum before the Scottish people. The bill was killed by a procedural clause when, in a modest turnout, just 1.23 million voted yes, barely outnumbering the 1.15 million who opposed it, and the Labour government fell shortly afterwards. Despite the outcome, discussion about the right of Scotland to have greater powers within the UK monopolised much of that session at Westminster.

The other surprising development has been the rise of the Scottish National Party from its most unpromising beginnings between the wars to a position where it rivals the other two main parties with its own elected representatives at Westminster – although as yet its hard core support is less consistent compared with theirs. On the other hand it gives positive indications of a movement that is here to stay, and its quest for greater respectability and wider popular support was boosted by successes in the 1994 local elections and a further seat in the European Parliament.

In spite of the seemingly impressive backing for the nationalist cause since the Second World War, its achievements can scarcely be called outstanding. Scotland has yet to achieve home rule – a distinct possibility immediately before the First World War – or a measure of devolved government, let alone the nationalists' goal of independence. With such frustrations of nationalist hopes one might expect the name of William Wallace – together with that of Bruce – to be brought before his countrymen as never before. This has scarcely been the case, for rallies at Elderslie have been sparsely attended and despite events such as the highly publicised theft of his great sword in 1972, Wallace has appeared to attract far less interest in the Scottish press and other media than formerly. This is despite the growing numbers of English and overseas visitors who attend his national monument and come away enthralled by his achievements, the publication of new biographies and even despite Mel Gibson's award-winning film.

Why is this so? It cannot be Wallace who has changed. He continues to represent what most Scots would acknowledge as their enduring virtues. Although he lived with the Scottish Catholic Church there was a Calvinistic intensity to his religious faith; his bravery and savagery marked him as someone incapable of irresolution, undue self-regard or accommodation with those he opposed; yet he also showed a gallant, ever-comradely, even sentimental, side to his nature. While for some it is his example as a man of principle undeterred by his enemy which is most significant, to the great majority of his countrymen his strongest image is that of a man who, above all, loved his country and hated unreservedly the threat which English interests posed to it.

However much homeland Scots might cherish such personal qualities in their hearts, in the late twentieth century they are apparently less important for success in the contemporary political environment. With their acceptance at Westminster, the political representatives of Scotland's National Party are now established figures with less need to keep quoting Wallace either as the arch rebel or definitive national leader. Perhaps this helps to explain why National MPs seem to favour another past hero, Fletcher of Saltoun, a Scottish parliamentarian like themselves, opposed to the conditions of the Union, although stopping short of Wallace's military rebellion. As Fletcher wrote at the end of the seventeenth century: 'I consider that, in a state of Separation from England my country would be perpetually involved in bloody and destructive wars . . . But if we should be united to that Kingdom in any other manner than by Federation, we must of necessity fall under the miserable and languishing condition of all places that depend on a remote seat of government.'[1]

The passage of time and the evolution of political and social systems are, of course, not irrelevant in the seeming neglect of Wallace. It has to be acknowledged that Wallace's ideal Scotland can never be equated with some of the Marxist luggage of the SNP, while his ideal was a monarchical system barely comparable with the democratic privilege enjoyed in present-day Scotland, independent or not. More important still than any such comparisons are the changes in individual attitudes within both England and Scotland in the centuries which have elapsed since the first wars of independence. The National MPs at Westminster no longer need to carry large swords or cover their bodies with armour: the votes given them at the ballot box are their most potent weapons and their best defence.

This is not all. If an unbiased reader from another planet had examined the leading articles which appeared in *The Scotsman* both during the run up to the 1979 referendum and to the 1992 General Election and had read the majority of its published letters, he would have been convinced that all red-blooded Scots were bound to support moves for greater independence. According to the paper's leader of 31 January 1992: 'No matter which party wins the election, reform that will change the historic constitutional arrangements of the last 300 years to a greater or lesser degree is certain.' As the election drew nearer, virtually any occurrence was interpreted as leading to the same end.

In the event, while many Scots flirted with the concept, when they came to the point of voting for greater independence, either through devolution or by more radical means, many held back at the last moment. Like all matters in Scotland any attempt to explain it seems to uncover new puzzles. A significant proportion from markedly different cultural regions were clearly unwilling to bring about a situation where the political running would be made by Strathclyde, their country's most populous district. They recognised, too, the risks for the formidable number of common practices on both sides of the border which had grown up over the 300 or so years of union, together with the mutual economic advantages. Yet it is also true that a considerable proportion of the Scottish people who had publicly demonstrated a strong desire for change were not prepared, when it came to the test, to face the unknown and the likelihood of confrontation.

In this respect the exploits of their country's heroes during the independence wars almost seven centuries ago, would seem to have a diminshed importance. To forecast future political developments is a hazardous process best left to political commentators. Yet it seems safe enough to suggest that over the next few years Scots are likely to have more opportunity to influence constitutional changes in their home country than at any other time since the days of the early revolutionary wars, certainly since 1707.

However, it would also be wrong to deny that, like most other countries, powerful and deep undercurrents exist in modern Scotland as they did in Wallace's Scotland 700 years ago. If by some unexpected political outcome hopes for such concessions are again frustrated and look likely to remain so over the medium term, it might arouse profound and potentially violent agitation like that practised by Wallace in his early days and akin to the exchanges between the republican and unionist communities in Northern Ireland. However, this seems most unlikely to happen. For while no one can doubt that Scotland, as a country, is still highly conscious of its traditions and its distinctness; that it takes an immense pride in the quality of its society, compared with other nations (including its southern neighbour); that it still produces great sons, not least in medicine, politics and law; it also has to be acknowledged that there is no longer the same urgency, level of energy and ambition that was the staple of the preceding two centuries.

The contemporary age, pragmatic and dominated by the need to support ageing populations and protect its environment, rather than seek ideological valhallas, appears to favour the more negative virtues, inclining towards preservation and safety rather than the traditional Scottish addiction to challenge and adventure. Full independence, rather than some greater say in internal affairs, can hardly be seen here as less than a precipitous leap into the unknown.

In 1992, shortly before the General Election, the author

attended a political meeting of the Scottish National Party held in the impressive Academy building at Avoch in Scotland's far north. Those attending did not, in the main, appear particularly disadvantaged or young. The main address painted a dazzling or a terrifying picture, according to one's political viewpoint, of a new Scotland with land, capital and mineral resources all placed under 'wise' central control. The oratory complete, there followed an opportunity for questions. The first questioner made no attempt to address such issues as the emergent country's place in Europe and beyond. His concern was quite clear: 'In the event of Scotland gaining its independence how would reciprocal national insurance and pension payments be handled with the rest of Britain?'

Most native Scots are doubtless far more adventurous than the questioner and remain high-principled, chivalrous, long-headed people, nationalistic, combatative and argumentative, with a deep unshakeable regard for their country's past history and traditions. Yet the prospect of increased powers leading to almost certain independence and with it the role of a small nation state within Europe, hardly seems to offer quite the same attraction as of old, or even of a few years ago. Economic recession on the Continent, increasing doubts about centralist measures and the opportunities offered outside Europe may have played their part. But to many independently-minded Scots there is the distinct possibility of European-inspired regulations falling more heavily upon some form of independent Scotland than the relatively indulgent diktats from Westminster. There is a genuine fear in some quarters that Edward I's tax collectors are reappearing in the guise of officials carrying rule books from Brussels. And in the last recession it should not be forgotten that it was Scotland, freed from the burden of heavy industry, that fared better than southern England.

Under such circumstances it is debatable whether the stark figure of William Wallace and the message of Burns (in the guise of an ardent nationalist seeking an independent Scotland) are as palatable as they were quite recently, even to the more radical elements. And the threats to Scottish national aspirations are no longer seen to come from England alone. At home Scottish inventiveness and energy in some ways seem less abundant then formerly: the great economic asset of North Sea oil is finite and, despite continuing finds in less accessible areas, not the source of infinite riches for the parent country which some expected. Again due to the passage of time and developments within the union, even the most revered Scottish institutions are no longer as distinctive as they once were. None the less, it is difficult to believe that the large numbers of Scots who occupy senior professional and managerial positions worldwide will falter for lack of mental tenacity or lack of principle. Yet different centuries undoubtedly have different standards, and the late twentieth century does, in some respects, appear inimical to the single-minded zeal of William Wallace, and for that matter to his great rival as well.

To future generations, Wallace might be viewed as a giant from another age: part of Scotland's tempestuous, colourful and much-cherished history who can fill the young with pride over his achievements. Alternatively, he might be reassessed as a national hero whose virtues and values can never be considered archaic. But in a world where clear messages were the exception, he could conceivably act as a bell-wether for national initiatives, whether towards pursuing new intellectual and commercial successes or towards the exercise of greater political influence.

NOTES

PROLOGUE

1 J. Fergusson, *William Wallace*, ix.
2 P. Abercromby, *Martial Achievements of the Scots Nation*, 2 vols, 1711, 1715.
3 G. Crawford, *The Peerage of Scotland* containing a Historical and Genealogical Account of the nobility of that Kingdom, 1716.
4 C. Rogers, *The Book of Wallace* (Stirling, 1889).
5 A. F. Murison, *Sir William Wallace* (London, 1898).
6 A. Fisher, *William Wallace* (Edinburgh, 1986).
7 D. J. Gray, *William Wallace, The King's Enemy* (London, 1991).
8 James Mackay, *William Wallace: Braveheart* (Edinburgh, 1995).

CHAPTER ONE

1 J. Major, *A History of Greater Britain* as well as England and Scotland compiled from the current authorities in 1521 (Scottish History Society, 1892), 205.
2 Blind Harry, *The Actis and Deidis of the Illustere and Vailzeand Campioun Schir William Wallace, Knicht of Ellerslie* (Scottish Text Society, 1889).
3 R. L. G. Ritchie, *The Normans in Scotland* (Edinburgh, 1954), 256–68.
4 I. D. Whyte, *Scotland before the Industrial Revolution*, (London, 1995), 26.
5 R. R. Davies, *Domination and Conquest: the experience of Ireland, Scotland and Wales* 1100–1300 (Cambridge, 1990).
6 G. W. S. Barrow, *The Beginnings of Feudalism in Scotland*. Bulletin of the Institute of Historical Research, xxix (1956), 1–31.
7 R. Nicolson, *Scotland, The Later Middle Ages* (Edinburgh, 1989).
8 G. W. S. Barrow, *Robert Bruce and the Community of the Realm of Scotland* (Edinburgh, 1988), 9.
9 Fergusson, *William Wallace*, 4.

CHAPTER TWO

1 T. Wright (ed.), *The Political Songs of England* (Camden Society, 1839), 93.
2 M. Prestwich, *Edward I* (London, 1988), 335.
3 Prestwich, *Edward I*, 205.
4 T. G. Tout, *Medieval Town Planning* (Manchester, 1934), 18.
5 R. Nicholson, *Scotland: The Later Middle Ages* (Edinburgh, 1989), 34.
6 Fergusson, *William Wallace*, 9.
7 E. L. G. Stones (ed.), *Anglo-Scottish Relations, 1174–1328: Some Selected Documents* (Oxford, 1965); Nicholson, *The Later Middle Ages*, 43.

CHAPTER THREE

1 Davies, *Domination and Conquest*, 51.
2 *The Chronicle of Lanercost 1272–1346*, trans. H. Maxwell (Glasgow, 1913), 163.
3 E. M. Barron, *The Scottish War of Independence* (Inverness, 1914), 33.
4 Johannis de Fordun, *Chronica Gentis Scotorum*, ed. W. F. Skene (Edinburgh, 1871–2), 321.
5 The Lanercost Chronicle put the Nativity of the Glorious Virgin as the point when (the people) began to show themselves in rebellion under William Wallace: *Chron. Lanercost* (Glasgow, 1913), 163.
6 It was commonplace at this time for many of the bishops to have sons who were usually referred to as their 'nephews'.

CHAPTER FOUR

1 Gray, *William Wallace*, 94.
2 J. E. Morris, *The Welsh Wars of Edward I* (Oxford, 1968), 283.
3 Fergusson, *William Wallace*, 34.
4 Fisher, *William Wallace*, 53.
5 Fergusson, *William Wallace*, 35.
6 Ibid, 39.
7 *Lanercost Chronicle* (Glasgow, 1913), 164.
8 *The Chronicle of Walter of Guisborough*, ed. H. Rothwell (Camden Society, 1957), 303.
9 P. F. Tytler, *The History of Scotland* (Edinburgh, 1864), i, 55.
10 *Chron. Lanercost* (Glasgow, 1913), 168.

11 *Johannis de Fordun, Chronica Gentis Scotorum*, ed. W.F. Skene (Edinburgh, 1871–2), xxviii.

12 Geoffrey Barrow points to an important instance where the Scottish feudal barons changed their allegiance. Those who went to Flanders served with Edward I against the French but when Edward was on his way home they joined the French king against him. As Barrow observes: 'In effect this can only mean that they joined Wallace.' Barrow, *Robert Bruce*, 137.

13 Walter Bower's *Scotichronicon*, ed. D.E.R. Watt et al, vi (Aberdeen, 1991), 83–4.

14 *Documents Illustrative of Sir William Wallace, his Life and Times*, ed. J. Stevenson (Maitland Club, 1841), 159 (with facsimile in frontispiece).

15 *Chron. Fordun*, 321–2.

16 Major, *A History of Greater Britain*, 198.

17 Bower, *Schotichronicon*, vi (Aberdeen, 1991), 87–8.

18 Barron, *The Scottish War of Independence*, 82–3.

19 Gray, *William Wallace*, 106.

CHAPTER FIVE

1 Morris, *Welsh Wars*, 286–93.

2 *Chron. Fordun*, 322.

3 Fergusson, *William Wallace*, 74.

4 Ibid, 76.

5 *Chron. Guisborough*, 324–5.

6 Ibid, 326.

7 Fergusson, *William Wallace*, 84.

8 J. F. C. Fuller, *Julius Caesar* (London 1965), 324.

9 *Chron. Bower*, vi, 97.

CHAPTER SIX

1 Stones, No. 33, *Anglo-Scottish Relations*.

2 *Chron. Fordun*, 321.

3 Barrow, *Robert Bruce*, 113.

4 Barrow, *Robert Bruce*, 104 n76.

5 Nicholson, *The Later Middle Ages*, 60.

6 Barrow, *Robert Bruce*, 114, citing *Chronicle Rishanger*, 447.

7 Barrow, *Robert Bruce*, citing Cal Docs Scot ii, No 1431.

8 Barrow, *Robert Bruce*, 165.

9 Barrow, *Robert Bruce*, 130; *Documents and Records illustrating the History of Scotland*, ed F. Palgrave (London 1837), 287.

10 *Flores Historiarum*, ed. H. R. Luard, iii (Rolls Series, 1890), 118.
11 Stevenson, *Wallace Docs*, 167.

CHAPTER SEVEN
1 A.M. Mackenzie, *Robert Bruce: King of Scots* (London, 1934), 117.
2 *Chron. Bower*, vi, 97.
3 Andrew of Wyntoun. *The Orygynale Cronykil of Scotland*, ed. D. Laing, iii (Edinburgh,1872), 348.
4 Ranald Nicolson, for instance, remarks that 'as a Scottish Cromwell he might have fashioned Scotland anew' (*Scotland: The Later Middle Ages*, 58).
5 Barrow, *Robert Bruce*, 115–16, 168.
6 Fergusson, *William Wallace*, 103.
7 Blind Harry, *Wallace*, Bk x, 960.
8 Ibid, 895.
9 Nicholson, *The Later Middle Ages*, 66.
10 Blind Harry, *Wallace*, Bk xi, 1105.
11 Fergusson, *William Wallace*, 110.
12 *Calendar of Documents Relating to Scotland*, ed. J. Bain (Edinburgh,1884), No. 1465.
13 Blind Harry, *Wallace*, Bk xi, 962.
14 Ibid, 1075.
15 Ibid, 1109.

CHAPTER EIGHT
1 Blind Harry, *Wallace*, xi, 1060.
2 Stevenson, *Wallace Documents*, 147.
3 Stevenson, *Wallace Documents*, Additional Manuscript, xxviii.
4 Stevenson, *Wallace Documents*, 193.
5 Blind Harry, *Wallace*, Bk xi, 1399.
6 Ibid, 1307.

CHAPTER NINE
1 Fergusson, *William Wallace*, 115.
2 Barron, *War of Independence*, 172.
3 Barrow, *Robert Bruce*, 161.
4 Nicholson, *The Later Middle Ages*, 76 (CDS, 11, No. 1926).

CHAPTER TEN
1 John Buchan's 'Montrose' (London, 1928) must rank as one of the great historical romances of the English language.

2 Mackenzie, *Robert Bruce*, 324.
3 *Chron Wyntoun*, 370.
4 Ibid, 549.
5 Major, *History of Greater Britain*, 195, 198.
6 *Letters of Robert Burns*, ed. Fergusson, i, 49–50.
7 Fergusson, *William Wallace*, 117.
8 Buchan, *Montrose*, 153.
9 W. Scott, *Tales of a Grandfather* (Edinburgh 1851), I, 48.
10 Fergusson, *William Wallace*, 119.
11 Barrow, *Robert Bruce*, 137–8.

CHAPTER ELEVEN
1 A. Marr, *The Battle for Scotland* (London 1992), 12.
2 J. M. Davidson, *Scotia Rediviva: Home Rule for Scotland* (London 1893).
3 Davidson, *Scotia Rediviva*, 105.
4 *Glasgow Herald*, Sept. 14 1909.
5 *Glasgow Herald*, 26 June 1911.
6 *Glasgow Herald*, 30 August 1920.
7 A. M. Mackenzie, *Scotland in Modern Times* 1720–1939 (London 1941), 278.
8 D. Young, *William Wallace and this War* (1943).
9 *Glasgow Herald*, 28 August 1944.

EPILOGUE
1 J. M. Davidson, *Scotland for the Scots* (1897), 69.

SELECT BIBLIOGRAPHY

The Actis and Deidis of the Illustere and Vailzeand Campioun Schir William Wallace, Knicht of Ellerslie (Scottish Text Society, 1889). [Blind Harry]

ABERCROMBY, Patrick. *Martial Achievements of the Scots Nation*, 2 Vols (Edinburgh 1711, 1715).

Andrew of Wyntoun, *The Orygynale Cronykil of Scotland*, ed. D. Laing (Edinburgh, 1872–9).

BAIN, D. *The Patriot, or Wallace* (London 1806).

BARBOUR, John. *The Bruce* (ed.) W. M. Mackenzie (London 1909).

BARRON, E.M. *The Scottish War of Independence* (Inverness 1934).

BARROW, G.W.S. *Robert Bruce and the Community of the Realm of Scotland*, 3rd ed. (Edinburgh 1988).

BARROW, G.W.S. *Scotland and its Neighbours in the Middle Ages* (London 1992).

BARROW, G.W.S. 'The Beginnings of Feudalism in Scotland', *Bulletin of the Institute of Historical Research*, xxix (1956), pp. 1–31.

BELL, I. *Robert Louis Stevenson: Dreams of Exile* (Edinburgh 1992).

BOWER, W. *Scotichronicon* (ed.) D. E. R. Watt et al (Aberdeen and Edinburgh 1987–91).

BROWN, J.T.T. *The Wallace and the Bruce Restudied* (London 1900).

BUCHAN, J. *Montrose* (London 1949).

BUTE, Marquis of, *The Early Days of Sir William Wallace* (London 1912).

Calendar of Documents Relating to Scotland 1108–1509 (ed.) J. Bain (Edinburgh 1881–8).

CAMERON LEES, J. *History of the County of Inverness* (Inverness 1847).

CARRICK, J.D. *Life of Sir William Wallace* (London 1858).

The Chronicle of Lanercost 1272–1346, translated by H. Maxwell (Glasgow, 1913).

The Chronicle of Walter of Guisborough, ed. H. Rothwell (Camden Society, 1957).

CRAWFORD, G. *The Peerage of Scotland Containing a Historical and Genealogical Account of the Nobility of that Kingdom* (Edinburgh 1716).

CUNNINGHAM, A. *Works of Robert Burns* (Boston 1836).

DAVIDSON, J.M. *Scotia Rediviva: Home Rule for Scotland* (1893).

DAVIES, R.R. *Domination and Conquest: the Experience of Ireland, Scotland and Wales 1100-1300* (Cambridge 1990).

Documents Illustrative of Sir William Wallace: His Life and Times, ed. J. Stevenson (Maitland Club, 1841).

Documents and Records Illustrating the History of Scotland, ed. F. Palgrave (London 1837).

DONALDSON, G. *Scottish Kings* (London 1967).

FERGUSSON, J. *William Wallace: Guardian of Scotland* (Stirling 1938).

FISHER, A. *William Wallace* (Edinburgh 1986).

Flores Historiarum, ed. H. R. Luard (Rolls Series, 1890).

Johannis de Fordun, *Chronica Gentis Scotorum*, ed. W. F. Skene (Edinburgh 1871–2).

FRAME, R. *The Political Development of the British Isles 1100-1400* (Oxford 1990).

FYFE, W.T. *Wallace: the Hero of Scotland* (London 1920; reprinted Edinburgh 1986).

GRANT, A. *Independence and Nationhood, Scotland 1306–1469* (London 1984).

GRAY, D.J. *William Wallace: The King's Enemy* (London 1991).

HARVIE, C. *Scotland and Nationalism 1707–1994* (London 1994).

The Life and Heroic Achievements of Sir William Wallace, the Scottish Patriot (Aberdeen 1842).

LYNCH, M. *Scotland: A New History* (London 1992).

MACKAY, J. *William Wallace: Braveheart* (Edinburgh 1995).

MACKENZIE, A.M. *Robert Bruce, King of Scots* (London 1934).

MACKENZIE, A.M. *Scotland in Modern Times* (London 1941).

MAJOR, John. A History of Greater Britain (Scottish History Society 1892).

MARR, A. *The Battle for Scotland* (London 1992).

MAXWELL, H.E. *The Early Chronicles Relating to Scotland* (London 1912).

MORRIS, J.E. *The Welsh Wars of Edward I* (Oxford 1968).

MURISON, A.F. *Sir William Wallace* (London 1818).

NICHOLSON, R. *Scotland: the Later Middle Ages* (Edinburgh 1978).

The Political Songs of England (ed.) T. Wright (Camden Society 1839).

PRESTWICH, M. *The Three Edwards* (London 1980).

PRESTWICH, M. *Edward I* (London 1988).

Proceedings at the Laying of the Foundation Stone of the National Wallace Monument (Edinburgh 1861).

RISHANGER, W. *Chronica et Annales* (ed.) M. T. Riley (London 1865).

RITCHIE, R.L.G. *The Normans in Scotland* (Edinburgh 1954).

RITCHIE, W.K. *Scotland in the Time of Wallace and Bruce* (London 1971).

ROGERS, C. *The Book of Wallace* (Stirling 1889).

SCOFIELD, W.H. *Mythical Bards and the Life of Sir William Wallace* (London 1970).

SCOTT, W. *Tales of a Grandfather* (Edinburgh 1851).

STONES, E.L.G.(ed.) *Anglo-Scottish Relations, 1174–1328: Some Selected Documents*, lst ed. (Oxford 1965).

TOUT, T.F. *Medieval Town Planning* (London 1934).

Traditions Respecting Sir William Wallace collected chiefly from publications of recent date by a former subscriber for a Wallace Monument (Edinburgh 1856).

WHYTE, I.D. *Scotland Before the Industrial Revolution* (London 1995).

YOUNG, D. *William Wallace and This War* (Private publication, 1943).

INDEX

Table of Scottish Kings

Name	Age at accession	Reign began	Reign ended	How ended	Length of reign
Malcolm II	50*	25th March 1005*	25th November 1034	Died	29 yrs 8 mths*
Duncan I "The Gracious"	33*	25th November 1034	14th August 1040	Murdered	5 yrs 8 mths
Macbeth	35*	14th August 1040	15th August 1057	Killed	17 yrs
Lulach "The Simple"	25*	15th August 1057	17th March 1058	Killed	7 mths
Malcolm III "Ceannmor"	27*	17th March 1058	13th November 1093	Killed	35 yrs 7 mths
Donald Bane (1st reign)	60*	13th November 1093	12th* May 1094	Deposed	6 mths*
Duncan II	34*	12th* May 1094	12th November 1094	Killed	6 mths*
Donald Bane (2nd reign)	61*	12th November 1094	8th* October 1097	Deposed	2 yrs 10 mths
Eadgar	23*	8th* October 1097	8th January 1107	Died	9 yrs 3 mths*
Alexander I "The Fierce"	31*	8th January 1107	23rd April 1124	Died	17 yrs 3 mths
David I "The Saint"	44*	23rd April 1124	24th May 1153	Died	29 yrs 1 mth
Malcolm IV "The Maiden"	11	24th May 1153	9th December 1165	Died	12 yrs 6 mths
William "The Lion"	22*	9th December 1165	4th December 1214	Died	48 yrs 11 mths
Alexander II	16	4th December 1214	8th July 1249	Died	34 yrs 7 mths
Alexander III	7	8th July 1249	19th March 1286	Killed	36 yrs 8 mths
Margaret "of Norway"	3*	19th March 1286	26th* September 1290	Died	4 yrs 6 mths
First Interregnum		*26th* September 1290*	*17th November 1292*		*2 yrs 1 mth*
John (Balliol)	42*	17th November 1292	10th July 1296	Abdicated	3 yrs 7 mths
Second Interregnum		*10th July 1296*	*27th March 1306*		*9 yrs 8 mths*
Robert I (Bruce)	31	27th March 1306	7th June 1329	Died	23 yrs 2 mths
David II (Bruce)	5	7th June 1329	22nd February 1371	Died	41 yrs 8 mths

* = approximate